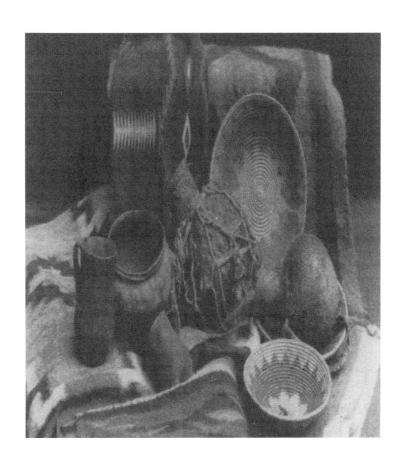

Native American Recipes from the Appalachian Mountains

AAIWV Tribal Cookbook

Compiled by:
Members of
Appalachian American Indians of West Virginia

6th Revised Edition

Appalachian American Indians of West Virginia

Appalachian American Indians of West Virginia, Inc. (AAIWV) is an intertribal tribe of Native Americans and their mixed-blood lineal descendants. Currently, we have over 5,000 members in West Virginia and surrounding states representing the bloodlines from 75 different Native American Tribes.

Consistent with the history of this area, the majority of our members share Cherokee or Shawnee ancestry, although tribes as distant as the Ojibwa, Seneca, and Apache are also represented. AAIWV is the largest Native American group in the State of West Virginia.

Chartered in 1989 as the Appalachian American Indian Society (a 501 (c) (3) corporation registered with the West Virginia Secretary of State) with 11 original members, we achieved state recognition as a tribal group on March 1, 1996 with the passage of Senate Resolution 25. This was followed by an identical resolution (House Resolution 19) passed by the House of Delegates on March 30, 2001.

The goals of AAIWV are to provide a "tribal home" for Native Americans in West Virginia, to save precious pieces of our heritage that are in danger of being lost and to educate both Native Americans and the general public about the history and culture of Native Americans in this state. We do this through extensive teaching activities throughout the state, by holding free powwows open to the public, and through meetings. We also publish a monthly newsletter, *The Appalachian Indian Voice*, which is distributed free to our members. AAIWV also provides assistance to our members in need with a small Food Pantry.

AAIWV is supported solely by the contributions of its members. We charge no fees or membership dues to our members.

AAIWV is governed by an elected Tribal Council consisting of a Principal Chief, Chief, Tribal Officer, Tribal Liaison, Secretary, Treasurer, and 15 Councilors.

Further information can be found on our website www.aaiwv-ani.org

Appalachian American Indians
A Timeline of the Historic Period

Prior to 1700	Shawnee and Mingo colonies claimed the eastern panhandle of what is now West Virginia and the southeastern area -- including the areas that are now Pocahontas and Greenbrier Counties. In 1670, there were known to be Cherokee as far north as the Kanawha Valley.
Around 1700	The Mingo moved south into what is now Logan County named after the Mingo chief Logan. In the northeastern counties were groups of Seneca, Tuscarora, Delaware, and Ottawa.
1701	Documents locate a Shawnee village site in Hardy County, WV. This was later abandoned when the Shawnee moved to what is now the Point Pleasant area and joined with the colony led by Chief Cornstalk.
1757	The Cherokee laid claim to all of the land south of the Kanawha River. The Shawnee largely moved with Chief Cornstalk's group to the area around what is now Xenia, OH and established a town called Hokolesque but still retained claim to the land north of the Kanawha River.
By 1760	Cherokee land claims were from the southern bank of the Kanawha River through Kentucky into Tennessee and south into Georgia and the Carolinas.
By 1760	Some Shawnee groups were also found in the southern states (as far south as Alabama) but later, most went back north into Kentucky and Ohio.
1820	Following Tecumseh's death in 1813. the Shawnee people who followed his movement began returning to homes in Kentucky, Ohio, Indiana, Illinois, and Virginia. Some lived with friendly Quaker and Amish families.
1830	The Indian Removal Act was passed calling for the relocation of all tribes to "Indian Territory" west of the Mississippi River. Under the terms of the Act, individuals were to be allowed to stay in their homes if they gave up all tribal claims and allegiance and agreed to become citizens of the states they lived in.

1832	The Treaty of 1832 called for the removal of all Shawnee to the west. The US government sent troops to forcibly remove Indians from Ohio and the Ohio River Valley if necessary. Some Shawnee families broke away from Chief Blue Jacket's group who was headed west and came into West Virginia south of the Kanawha River and into Kentucky and hid among the Cherokee who still lived in the area. Some stayed with "mixed blood" relatives who were a significant part of the population. Although the major Cherokee population centers at this time were in Tennessee, northern Georgia, and Arkansas, some families broke with the main Cherokee body and moved back into the hills of the Carolinas and Virginia (now West Virginia). Many "mixed-blood" families of Cherokee, Shawnee, and English/Scots/Irish heritage were formed at this time.
1835	The Treaty of New Echota was signed selling all Cherokee Tribal lands east of the Mississippi River to the US government. (This treaty was signed by a small group of Cherokee and was invalid. The treaty was a violation of Cherokee law that made the sale of Tribal lands without Tribal approval a capital offense. Most of the members of the "Treaty Party" were subsequently killed by Cherokee vigilantes, setting off a civil war among the Cherokees in Indian Territory.)
1837-1838	The Trail of Tears -- Federal troops under General Winfield Scott rounded up the Cherokees in Tennessee, Georgia, and the Carolinas. Some Cherokees in the Carolinas (under Chief Yonaguska [Drowning Bear]) resisted and went into hiding in the hills. The Cherokees in North Carolina were later given amnesty by Winfield Scott and their descendants live there on the "Quallah Boundary" to this day as the Eastern Band of Cherokee. Cherokee and Shawnee living in Virginia and Kentucky were not moved at this time since Scott didn't have enough men to bother with the relatively small number of people living on land most white settlers didn't want. Thousands of those who did travel the Trail of Tears died along the trail of starvation, disease, and exposure. Estimates of the total deaths from this forced march range from one-in-four and one-in-three.
1863	Founding of West Virginia. West Virginia was officially a "segregated state" with racial lists of all inhabitants. Many Native American and "mixed blood" families were identified as "white" or "colored" on the census. "Indians", by law, did not exist and it was not legal to register a child as "Indian" at birth. Indians were also prohibited by law from owning property in West Virginia as identified "Indians".

1890	Documentation by the American Bureau of Ethnography and the US Census places "pocket communities" of Cherokee in Logan, Mingo, Summers, Monroe, Greenbrier, Clay, and Fayette Counties. There were also Shawnee living in these communities. Eastern Blackfoot were located in Roane County.
1894	Documented Shawnee "pocket community" in Mason County.
1902	Shawnee communities were identified in Braxton, Clay, McDowell, Fayette, Mason, Mingo, and Kanawha Counties. The largest Shawnee community appears to have been on the Little Kanawha River.
1940s-1970s	Federal government policy was to move Indians off the western reservations to find work in the cities and in other parts of the country. Families of many different tribal lineages settled in West Virginia, Kentucky, Virginia, and Ohio. Many families of Lakota, Pawnee, Seneca, and other tribes settled in our area during these years.
1965	Following the 1964 Civil Rights Act, the West Virginia legislature passed state laws that fully enfranchised all citizens. It was again legal for Native Americans to own land in West Virginia and to indicate Native American ancestry on birth records.
1989	The Appalachian American Indian Society was formed. This subsequently became Appalachian American Indians of West Virginia. The group was formally recognized by the West Virginia Legislature in 1996 and 2001.

Carla Ponder

Note about recipes: The recipes included within this book have been contributed by members of Appalachian American Indians of West Virginia. Some are traditional recipes. Others are modern adaptations of traditional recipes and some are modern. As one of our Elders, Talking Leaves, has stated many times. "We, as Indian people, adapt. That is how we have survived." So, please feel free to adapt and experiment. If you would like a "traditional" dish, try substituting indigenous foods in the recipes such as Jerusalem artichokes for potatoes or ramps for garlic. Have fun. Feast well!

FOOD FACTS

Fully two-thirds of all foodstuffs now being consumed were under cultivation in North America – and no where else in the world – before Columbus set foot on Hispaniola. Elaborate and sophisticated agricultural technologies had been achieved – some by men; others by women – and had been brought to perfection by the Indians.

A few of these were: Intricate and highly efficient irrigation systems (some are still in use today); cross-pollination (to increase the yield and to acclimatize the plants); clearing undergrowth (enticing much needed game to forage nearby): planting orchards near communal gardens (so game would eat the fruit instead of the vegetables); crop rotation (letting the land lie fallow); and the refinement of botanical experimentation facilities.

SOME WEST VIRGINIA INDIAN FOOD PLANTS

Potatoes	Peppers	Greens	Turnips
Tomatoes	Amaranth	Pawpaws	Peanuts
Squash	Pignuts	Chestnuts	Butternuts
Artichokes	Sunflowers	Strawberries	Chinquapins
Pumpkins	Corn	Blackberries	Mustard
Black Walnuts	Acorns	Wild Carrot	Ramps

SOME WEST VIRGINIA INDIAN FOOD ANIMALS

Bison	Turkey	Opossum	Elk
Deer	Rabbit	Muskrat	Mink
Beaver	Raccoon	Chipmunk	Squirrel
Geese	Bear	Ducks	Pheasant
Grouse	Skunk	Quail	Pigeon

FRESH WATER FOODS

Trout	Catfish	Clams	Bass
Oysters	Sunfish	Blue Gills	Crayfish
Cattails	Wild Rice	Lilies	

What was the Indian's toothbrush? A twig from a Birch Tree.

Before measuring cups and spoons:

1 cup –   the amount of liquid or dry ingredient that would fill a
               medium-sized bison horn

Handful –   amount that could be scooped up in one's hand

1 finger –   **amount that could be scooped up in the crook of one's little
               finger**

2 or 3 fingers – amount that could be scooped up by either 2 or 3 fingers
               while holding little finger down with thumb

Spices and Seasonings: The Indian's taste buds, unaltered by artificial

ingredients, knew when foods tasted "flat." The needed extra's were
obtained from a variety of dried or green plants, seeds, bark, leaves, and
roots.

Salt   from salt licks. It was also obtained from plants, such as
             coltsfoot. The dried leaves were pulverized and burnt. The
             ashes were then used as salt.

Pepper   Many varieties of peppers grew in North America, including
             red, yellow, green, hot, and mild.

Vinegar   made by fermenting the sap of the Sugar Maple or the Birch
             trees.

Mints   Several varieties of peppermint, spearmint, and wintergreen
             were used.

Baking Powder a leavening agent obtained by roasting the bones of
               animals to produce calcium carbonate.

Meal/flour   from nuts, corn, grain, seeds, pumpkins, or tubers,
               which were dried, ground, then sifted. Acorns were
               leached of acid before using. The meals and flours

were used for breads or as a thickening agent for stews.

Sugar   was obtained from boiling down the sap of the Sugar Maple or Birch trees, or sugar cane. Honey was a special treat.

Preserving Foods:

By Talking Leaves and Little Flower

Indians preserved foods by three primary methods: drying, smoking and salting.

Northwestern and coastal tribes preserved salmon, shee, and other fish by sun drying on racks and by drying and smoking over slow-burning fires long before the white man came to these shores. Smoked salmon today is only a little different than the earlier version. It is still a real delicacy among Natives and newcomers alike.

Eastern Indians smoked meats over smoldering cornhusks and over woods such as sassafras, hickory, and fruit woods. The fires were little more than glowing embers in order to generate as much smoke and as little heat as possible. Vegetables such as corn and beans were usually sun-dried on woven racks as were some fruits.

My family smoked practically all of our pork for the winter and some folks smoked a few pieces of beef. The smoking process was preceded by a drying process, with the meat usually being buried in a thick covering of coarse salt to hasten the drying.

We dried apples and a few other fruits, green beans and shell beans and our real staple, corn. The dried fruits and vegetables were reconstituted by boiling and then prepared in the usual way. The drying process varied only slightly. The sweet corn was cut from ears and the ears scraped with the back side of a table knife to recover the tiny parts of kernels left from the cutting. We didn't waste any precious food. It was too hard to come by. The cut kernels were spread on a tin pan or sheet and the drying process hastened by placing them in the oven of our wood-burning stove. We sometimes dried them in the warming closet, which perched atop every decent cook stove back then. When fully dried, the corn was placed in sealed containers until we needed it for use.

Wild Foods:

By Talking Leaves and Little Flower

There are dozens of wild foods which were used by Indians. It would be difficult to list all of them and any listing might lead to trouble if the reader did not know his wild plants. There are a few which are difficult to confuse with any other and which most folks already know from close encounters of the eating or pesty kind.

Ramps (Wa s di) -- The ramp is a wild leek. It nearly always bears two broad green leaves which can reach about a foot in height. The nearest look alike in our woods is adder's tongue, which has spotted leaves and an early-blooming yellow flower. Ramps develop a circular compound flower about the size of a half-dollar having several tiny white blossoms at the ends of the radii. If you are in doubt, sniff the crushed leaves or bulb. It smells stronger than garlic. Eat raw or cooked.

Artichokes (Gu ge) -- a.k.a. today as Jerusalem Artichokes. *Helianthus tuberosus.* (Sunflower Family) We have seen vast patches of this tall (up to 6 feet) plant with the yellow flower at the top which were probably planted by early Natives. They cultivated the plant long before the white man came and a few of those patches have remained virtually undisturbed. It grows from southern Canada into the south. The leaves are long, broad, thick, hard and hairy, and grow alternately on the upper stem and often opposite on the lower stem which is also rough and hairy. Indians dug the roots, peeled and ate them raw.

Dandelions -- Called by more names than you can shake a fist at, especially by lawn happy residents. Leaves can be eaten raw or cooked. Roots were boiled and used for medicine or tonic. Blossoms can be eaten raw or cooked. Steam blossoms and drip melted butter through them. Blossoms were also used to make a potent alcohol-rich wine that would clear all your pipes and maybe some of your neighbor's. Cut the serrate leaves near the stem, clean well, use as salad or cook by parboiling for about 5 minutes, drain, then boil until tender. Season with bacon grease and salt to taste. Dandelions were our first green vegetable of spring, but because of the slightly bitter taste we soon found other wild greens to help fill our pots, both the iron one and the flesh-covered one. Watch out for fall-out from all sources as you pick, especially if your yard isn't fenced.

Table of Contents

Navajo Country

Emerald Juniper mounds
dot sorrel plains.
Red cliff mesas
guard the horizon,
like lines of Mohican haircuts.

Among the high rocks,
shape shifted
by wind,
spirits whisper.

One-room log hogans,
shelter against scorpions,
mountain lions, rattle snakes,
hug bronze earh. Outhouses,
painted red and brown,
blend against mesas.

Stooped and leathered,
a woman pats frybread
over an outdoor fire.
In hot grease, the flat dough
rises like plate-sized biscuits,
and she keeps it warm
in paper bags.

Brown children ride
speckled ponies bareback.
A young woman, her raven hair
falling like shimmering water,
etches pottery in turquoises and corals.
As the red sun nestles into dessert sand,
children play among junipers, knowing
every Hogan is open, home.

Like hovering smoke signals,
clouds promise rain
to cracked earth.
Sheep cross rutted roads
at will, searching gullies
for spring water.
Then floods wash mesas,
clean out gullies,
widen ruts.

After rain,
sage perfumes the valleys;
Navajo tea springs
from gullies, its yellow
spike a beacon to gatherers.

The people take
what the earth gives
and says it is enough.

Delilah Conley O'Haynes

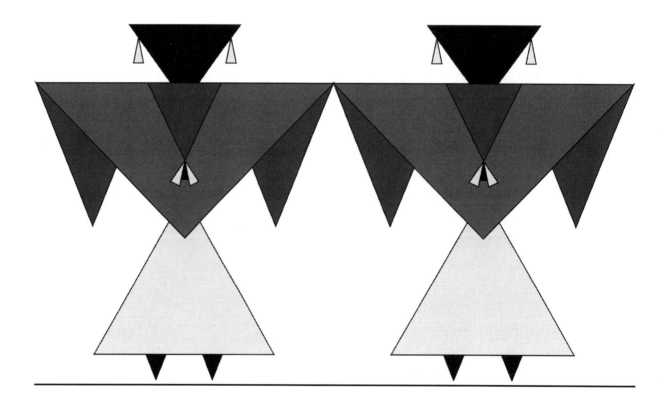

SOUPS

ABENAKI BEAN SOUP

1/2 lb. soup beans, dried
4 large potatoes
4 Tbs. salt
1/2 c. shallots, chopped

1/2 lb. black beans
4 Tbs. oil
1/2 tsp. black pepper

Wash, soak, and cook the dried beans. Retain the cooking water. Cook the potatoes and save the cooking water. Measure the reserved cooking waters to 8 cups. Add fresh water if necessary. Pour cooking water into soup pot. Crush beans and potatoes and add to the liquid. Add salt, oil, pepper, and shallots. Simmer slowly for 1 hour.

PUEBLO PINTO BEAN SOUP

3 15-oz. cans pinto beans
1 medium onion
1/2 tsp. black pepper
3 cloves garlic, minced
1 c. cubed cooked ham

2 16-oz cans chicken broth
1 c. corn (optional)
1/2 tsp. ground coriander
1/2 red chile pod (no seeds)
Salt and pepper to taste

In large skillet or Dutch oven, sauté onion in oil or butter until clear. Stir in all other ingredients. Simmer on medium heat, stirring occasionally until flavors are well blended, about 35 minutes. Serves 4-6.

BEANS WITH HOMINY

1 1/2 c. dried Anasazi beans
10 c. water
3 c. dried hominy

1 1/2 c. dried pinto beans
1 tsp. salt

Soak beans overnight in enough water to cover. Rinse beans with cold water and place in a large pot with fresh water to cover. Stir in salt. Cover and simmer slowly 2 to 2-1/2 hours until beans are tender. Add water when necessary, stirring to prevent beans from scorching. Add hominy and simmer, covered, for 1 hour, stirring occasionally.

BERRY SOUP

1 1/2 lbs. chuck steak, boned and trimmed   3 Tbs. peanut oil
1 medium white onion, sliced   2 c. beef stock
1 c. blackberries   1 Tbs. honey
Salt to taste

Broil steak in oven until brown on both sides. Set meat aside to cool. In large, heavy pot, heat oil and brown the onions. Cut the meat into bite-sized pieces and add to the pot. Add the blackberries and enough beef stock to barely cover the meat. Stir in the honey and simmer, covered, until meat is tender, about 1 hour. If the berries are too tart, add more honey to taste.

LAKOTA BUFFALO STEW

Buffalo stew meat, medium chunks
Wild turnips, diced
Onions, sliced

In a large pot, put in buffalo meat, onions, and turnips. Add water. Cover and boil until done. Season as desired.

BUFFALO VEGETABLE STEW

2 lbs. buffalo   1/4 c. oil
2 large onions, chopped   2 cloves garlic, minced
2 c. corn   8 c. water
1 tsp. salt   1 tsp. oregano
1/2 tsp. pepper   4 carrots, sliced
3 potatoes, cubed   1 green pepper (optional)

Cut buffalo in cubes. Brown in oil. Put meat aside and sauté garlic and onions in the buffalo oil. Return the meat into pan. Add water, corn, salt, and pepper. Cook for 2 hours or until meat is tender. Add the vegetables and continue to cook until done, about 30 minutes.

GAME STEW

2 lbs. cubed moose, elk, or deer	1/3 c. maple syrup
4 c. water	Salt to taste
4 green onions, sliced	4 white turnips, peeled and
diced	
4 medium potatoes, diced	1 leek, chopped

Place meat on skewers and sear over an open fire or brown in a large skillet. Place browned meat and remaining ingredients in a large pot. Simmer over an open fire or on the stove over medium-low heat for 1 hour or until meat is tender.

CLOVER SOUP

2 c. clover flowers and leaves	1 onion, chopped
3 Tbs. butter	4 c. water
3 potatoes, peeled and quartered	Salt & pepper, to taste
Parsley	Grated cheese, of choice

Clean and dip clover flowers and leaves in cold salt water. Remove from the water and cut these into pieces. In a large saucepan, sauté flowers, leaves, and chopped onion in butter. After all have softened, add water, then potatoes, and season with salt and pepper. Cook gently for 20 minutes. Drain the cooking liquid and save it. Puree the potato-clover-onion mixture. Then, add the reserved cooking liquid. Stirring constantly, bring this to a boil, then reduce heat and simmer for 3 minutes. Garnish with parsley and sprinkle with grated cheese.

CORN SOUP #1

Cook corn in water with bits of meat, wild edible greens such as dandelions, cowslip, or milkweed, and wild rice.

FISH SOUP #1

Fish, of any kind	Coarse cornmeal
Wild onions and wild greens	

Boil fish in pot. Add cornmeal to make soup of suitable consistency. Add onions and greens. Simmer and serve hot.

CORN SOUP #2

Soak dried corn in hot water containing 1 tablespoon of lye until the kernels are soft and the corn's hard shell is coming loose, and then drain and wash the soft corn with water to remove the lye and separate the hulls. In a separate pot, render down a hunk of salt pork or fatback. Add diced onions and fry until the onions are transparent then add the corn and water. Heat to boiling then lower heat and simmer for 1 hour or until done. Some people add milk for a creamy soup but care must be taken to avoid scalding the milk.

AUNTIE PAT'S CORN SOUP

1 piece salt pork, dice small and render it in a frying pan—cook really well. Add good size diced onion and cook until transparent.
Add a couple of diced potatoes (small) and cover with water. Cook until potatoes are about done.
Add:
2 cans evaporated milk
2 cans of creamed corn
Cook over low heat--just simmer for 30 minutes to 1 hour---don't boil.
Serve hot.

Pat Hahn

MOHAWK CORN SOUP

2 lbs. chuck beef, cubed about 1" about 1"	1 lb. pork, no bones, cubed
1 c. carrots	3 tsp. salt
1 tsp. pepper	2 c. canned or cooked kidney beans
8 c. canned hominy, drained	8 c. water
1 c. diced yellow turnip (optional)	

Cover beef and pork with 8 cups water. Cook with a little salt for 1-1/2 hours or until tender. Add remaining ingredients. Simmer 1 hour.

NOTE: 1 c. chopped cabbage may be added in place of the turnips, but either is optional.

ONEIDA CORN SOUP

1 c. fresh spinach, torn
1 c. beef, cooked and cut in small pieces
1 qt. water
Pepper, to taste

2 c. whole kernel corn
1/2 c. long grain rice
3 Tbs. wild rice

Mix in medium pot. Simmer until rice is cooked, about 25 – 30 minutes.

PAWNEE INDIAN CORN SOUP

Stew size beef chunks
Salt & black pepper
Onions

Dried corn
Potatoes

For the amount of soup you want to make, take stew-sized beef chunks and cut them in half. You can use ground beef, 80%+, in place of the beef chunks. Boil water for the amount of soup you want to prepare. When the water is at boiling point, drop in the determined amount of beef chunks or ground beef. Add salt and pepper to taste. Boil meat until the broth has a brownish color. While the meat is boiling, add the raw onions and raw potatoes. After the broth has reached the brownish color, add the quantity of dried corn you wish to cook. Cook for at least 30 to 45 minutes until the corn is soft and tender. The dried corn will absorb the beef flavor as it cooks. You can serve the corn soupy as a meal or drain the soup and serve the corn and beef as a side dish.

CORN CHOWDER

1 c. each chopped onion and celery
5 small potatoes, cooked
4 c. milk
4 c. white cornmeal, cooked

2 Tbs. butter
1 c. diced ham (optional)
4 c. yellow cornmeal, cooked
Salt and pepper, to taste

Cook onions and celery in butter until tender. Add Potatoes, ham, milk, and corn. Cover and simmer 15 Min, Do not boil. Stir frequently. Season with salt and pepper.

Mary Ann Neal (Windtalker)

STORM'S CORN CHOWDER

1/2 lb. bacon, cut up

2 stalks celery, chopped

4 c. milk

1 can cream-style corn
   diced

1 can diced tomatoes

Paprika, to taste

1 medium onion, chopped

2 Tbs. all-purpose flour

1/8 tsp. pepper

1 can small, whole potatoes,

Snipped, fresh parsley

Grated cheese

Cook bacon in a 3-qt. saucepan until crisp. Drain, reserving 3 tablespoons fat in the saucepan. Cook and stir onion and celery in bacon fat until tender. Remove from heat and stir in flour. Cook over low heat, stirring constantly until the mixture is bubbly. Remove from heat. Stir in milk. Heat to boil, stirring constantly. Boil and stir for 1 minute. Stir in salt, pepper, corn, tomatoes, and potatoes. Heat thoroughly. Stir in bacon. Sprinkle each serving with parsley, paprika, and grated cheese.

Heather Storm Stone

CHOCTAW HOMINY SOUP

1/4 lb. salt pork, cut in small pieces

58 oz. canned hominy, drained

1/2 tsp. salt

1 medium yellow onion, sliced

1 qt. buttermilk

1/4 tsp. pepper

Fry pork salt thoroughly and drain. Add onion to drippings and sauté slowly until golden and transparent. Mix in hominy and heat gently for 5 minutes. Add buttermilk, salt, and pepper. Heat very slowly for 5 minutes.

POTATO SOUP

Peel white potatoes and cut into small pieces. Boil in water with an onion or two until potatoes and onions mash easily. After mashing, add some fresh milk and reheat mixture. Add salt and pepper to taste.

CONNUCHE

Beat so hi (hickory nuts) very fine. Using a little water, form into balls (about the size of a softball) that include both shells and nutmeats. Each ball should prepare food for 20 persons.   Depending upon how many your are feeding, take a portion of the ball and place it in a saucepan. Cover it with boiling water. Stir well separating the shells from the meat. Strain through a cloth or fine sieve. Add rice, hominy, mushrooms, or venison pieces, whatever you prefer. Simmer until added ingredients are done.

CHICKEN STEW

1 frying chicken
1/2 c. potatoes, diced
1/4 c. onions, diced
Salt and pepper, to taste

1/2 c. corn kernels
1/2 c. tomatoes, diced
1/2 c. lima beans

Cut frying chicken in pieces, then brown in a deep pan. Cover with water and simmer 1 hour. Add other ingredients and simmer 20 minutes longer. Remove chicken from pot and de-bone it. Return meat to stew, reheat, and serve hot. Season with salt and pepper to taste.

HAZELNUT SOUP

24 oz. hazelnuts, crushed
3 Tbs. parsley, chopped
1 tsp. salt

6 shallots, with tops
6 c. stock
1/4 tsp. black peppe

Place all ingredients in a large pot and simmer slowly over medium heat for 1 1/2 hours, stirring occasionally.
NOTE: Vegetable, beef, venison or chicken stock may be used.

YELLOW JACKET SOUP

Gather ground-dwelling yellow jackets whole comb early in the morning. Place insects over heat (right- side up) to loosen grubs, and then remove them. Place comb over heat again until the cover parches. Remove and pick out the yellow jackets and brown them in a 350° F. oven. Make soup by boiling in water. Season to taste with grease and salt.

FISH CHOWDER

1 c. chopped onion
1 tsp. salt
5 c. raw fish, 3/4" cubes
2 c. milk
Parsley or chives

4 c. cubed potatoes
1/8 tsp. pepper
1 qt. boiling water
1 c. Half & Half® cream

Add potatoes, onions, salt, and pepper to water. Cook about 10 minutes until the vegetables are soft, but not completely cooked. Add fish and cook 10 minutes. Add milk and cream. Stir and heat 15 minutes longer. DO NOT BOIL. Serve with parsley or chives.

FISH SOUP #2

4 large mushrooms, sliced consommé
2 Tbs. yellow cornmeal
1 clove garlic, crushed
1 onion, thinly sliced
1/4 tsp. salt
10 oz. baby lima beans

2 10-1/2-oz. cans beef

2 Tbs. minced parsley
1/2 tsp. basil
Dash of fresh ground pepper
1 lb. haddock fillets
1/3 c. dry sherry (optional)

Place the mushrooms, consommé, cornmeal, parsley, garlic, basil, onion, pepper, and salt in a large saucepan and simmer, uncovered for 10 minutes. Add haddock, lima beans, and sherry. Simmer 20 minutes, stirring occasionally, breaking haddock into bite-sized pieces. Serve hot.

PUMPKIN SOUP

1 large pumpkin

1/2 stick of butter

2 Tbs. curry powder

1 Tbs. sea salt

2 Tbs. vanilla extract (or the real thing)

3 qts. milk

2 medium onions

1 c. sugar

2 tsp. pumpkin pie spice

4 dashes Tabasco®

Cut 1/5 of the pumpkin at the top and clean seeds for slow-baking later. Place pumpkin and its lid into oven at about 225 ° F. for about 2 hours. After cooling, scrape out inside pulp being careful not to break the skin of the pumpkin.

Pulverize pulp. Slice the onions and sauté in butter. In a separate kettle, cook the remaining ingredients at low heat less than 10 minutes. Turn off the heat and add the pumpkin pulp and remaining ingredients then heat slowly to about 180° F. but do not boil. Serve hot or cold in the pumpkin shell.

EagleClaw Parkins

RAMPS

Ramps (Cherokee= wa s' di) are a relative of the wild onion and garlic. They have been used since long before the European settlers arrived as a spring tonic. They are particularly good in the spring when they are tender and mild. West Virginia is the home of several festivals to honor ramps. Ramp festivals always feature fried ramps with everything from scrambled eggs to steaks.

RAMP SOUP

2 qt. salted water

40 ramps (wild leeks), divided

3 carrots

4 Tbs. butter or margarine

1 lb. stew beef, cut in chunks

5 stalks celery

1 lb. potatoes

Combine salted water and beef in large saucepan; boil for 15 minutes. Remove any scum that forms. Dice and add to the water 20 ramps, celery, carrots, and potatoes. Simmer for 2-1/2 hours. Remove meat and keep warm. In a frying pan, sauté remaining ramps in butter or margarine until tender. Add 1 cup water and vegetable mixture. Simmer for 10 minutes. Put the two leek mixtures through a sieve or food mill and serve hot in a soup bowl, accompanied by the meat.

NOTE: This mountain recipe is from the Richwood, WV Ramp Festival.

RAMP SOUP (RAMP VISCHYSSOISE)

4 bunches of ramps (handfuls), diced with leaves
2 lbs. southern hash brown potatoes or 4 pounds of potatoes, diced
1 stick butter
3 qt. milk
Salt and white pepper to taste
2 oz. olive oil

Sauté ramps in butter then sauté potatoes in olive oil.   Combine with milk, salt, and pepper. Heat to 180° F. but do not boil. Serve hot or cold.

VEGETABLE SOUP

1 green pepper, diced	3 Tbs. oil
1/2 cucumber, diced	10 shallots, diced
16 oz. green peas, cooked	16 oz. corn
16 oz. tomatoes, crushed mashed	1 c. Jerusalem artichokes,
Grilled bannock	Salt and pepper, to taste

Fry the pepper, cucumber, and shallots in the oil until tender. Add peas, corn, tomatoes, artichokes, and bannock. Season to taste. Stir and heat. NOTE: Potatoes can be used in the place of the artichokes.

TUSCARORA YELLOW SQUASH SOUP

1 medium yellow squash, diced

4 c. water

5 1/2-inch thick slices of cucumber

1/4 tsp. black pepper

4 shallots, with tops, chopped

2 Tbs. maple syrup

1 Tbs. salt

Place squash, shallots, water, and syrup in a large soup pot and simmer for 40 minutes until squash is tender. Add cucumbers. Pour everything into large mixing bowl and mash until it forms a thick, creamy paste. Pour paste back into pot. Season with salt and pepper. Simmer for 5 - 10 minutes.

STEW

Stews were made by throwing into the pot (animal skins, in this instance) whatever was indigenous to the area and letting it simmer all day. Sometimes, if meat was in short supply, it was simply a vegetarian stew. If the tribe lived near the seacoast, they made fish, clam, or lobster chowder. Dumplings were used to thicken stews. Usually, stew was made when they were either busy trying to cut, cure, and preserve their vegetables, herbs, roots, and meats and the season had blessed them with more than they could work with without allowing it to spoil. It was a good time for the entire village or town to have a feast. Stew was also made at the end of winter when they were cleaning out the larders in preparation for the coming spring.

In this area, the commonly used ingredients were:

Potatoes	Tomatoes	Carrots	Lima Beans
Celery	Turnips	Parsley	Barley
Cabbage	Peppers	Corn	Peas
Venison	Beef	Ham	Chicken
Spices and seasonings of your choice			

Put it all in a big pot. Cover it with water. Season to taste. Push it to the back of the stove. Stir occasionally and let simmer all day while you go about your business. Nothing tops it off like a pan of hot cornbread, scallions, and fresh buttermilk.

CHEROKEE PEPPER POT SOUP

1 lb. venison or beef short ribs or shanks
2 large onions, quartered
1 large bell pepper, diced
1/2 c. diced potatoes
1/2 c. fresh or frozen corn kernels
Salt & ground pepper, to taste

2 qt. water
2 ripe tomatoes, diced
1 c. fresh or frozen okra
1/2 c. sliced carrots
1/4 c. chopped celery

Put meat, water, and onions in a heavy soup kettle. Cover and bring to a boil over high heat. Reduce heat to low and simmer for 3 hours. Remove meat. Let cool, then discard bones. Return meat to pot. Stir in remaining vegetables and simmer for 1-1/2 hours. Season with salt and pepper. Serves 4 – 6.

VENISON AND WILD RICE STEW

3 1/2 lbs. shoulder of venison, cut into 2" cubes
2 tsp. salt
Pepper to taste
2 qt. water
2 large onions, peeled and quartered
1 1/2 c. wild rice, washed in cold water

Put venison, water, and onions in a large pot. Simmer uncovered for 3 hours. Add salt, pepper, and wild rice. Cover and simmer for 20 minutes. Stir well. Simmer uncovered for another 20 minutes, or until rice is tender and most of the liquid is absorbed.

WILD BOAR STEW

3/4 lb. wild boar, hind quarters, cut into 2" cubes

2 tsp. salt

Ground pepper, to taste

2 1/2 qt. water

2 medium yellow onions, peeled and quartered

2 ribs celery, sliced into 1" pieces

2 carrots, sliced into 1" pieces

2 Tbs. apple cider vinegar, or more to taste

3 Tbs. flour

3 Tbs. lard or shortening

Place cut up meat into a large heavy kettle. Add salt, pepper, and water.
Simmer uncovered for 25 minutes, skimming the foam off the top. Add
onions, celery, and carrots. Bring to boil, reduce heat, cover and cook over
low heat for 2-3 hours or until meat is tender. Add vinegar. Stir well.
Remove from heat and set aside for 2-3 hours. Skim off fat. In a small
saucepan, combine flour and lard and cook, stirring often, until golden
brown. Add 1 cup cooking liquid or water if the liquid has cooked down too
much. Whisk until smooth. Add to the meat, bring to boil. Reduce heat
and simmer, stirring occasionally, until slightly thickened.

BUTTERNUT SQUASH SOUP WITH ROASTED PUMPKIN SEEDS

2 large butternut squashes, skin and seeds removed, cut into 2-inch pieces

Salt

Honey

1/4 c. pumpkin seeds

Chopped chives

Place squash meat into a heavy saucepan and cover with water. Cook until
tender. Drain, reserving liquid. Place some of the squash in a food
processor and process until smooth, adding some of the reserved liquid to
thin if necessary. Season with salt and sweeten with honey to taste.
Place pumpkin seeds on a baking sheet in at 350° oven and roast until
fragrant.

Ladle soup into warm bowls and garnish with chives and pumpkin seeds.

THREE SISTERS STEW

1 Tbs. olive or canola oil	1 large onion, sliced
1 jalapeno chili, finely chopped	4 c. yellow summer squash,
sliced	
4 c. zucchini, cut in 1-inch pieces	4 c. butternut squash, peeled
and	
3 c. green beans, cut in 1-inch pieces	cubed
1 c. whole kernel corn	1 tsp. thyme
1 16-oz. cans kidney beans, undrained	

Heat oil in Dutch oven or soup pot over medium heat. Cook onion and chili in the hot oil for 2 minutes, stirring occasionally, until onion is tender. Stir in remaining ingredients. Cover over low heat, stirring frequently until squash is tender.

NO-MEAT CHILI

1 c. dried pinto or kidney beans	Water
1 Tbs. vegetable oil	2 c. chopped onion
1 green bell pepper, chopped	2 c. tomatoes, diced
1 6-oz. can tomato paste	3/4 c. water
3 Tbs. chili powder	1 Tbs. vinegar
1 tsp. oregano	1/2 tsp. black pepper
1 bay leaf	1 Tbs. sugar

Soak beans overnight. Drain. Cover with water and cook until tender. Drain and set aside. Heat oil in large Dutch oven or stockpot over medium-high heat. Add onion and pepper. Cook until onion is tender. Add beans and remaining ingredients. Bring to a boil, then reduce heat. Simmer, stirring occasionally. Add water if chili becomes too thick. Remove bay leaf before serving.

CHILI STEW FOR 35

10 lbs. stew beef

2 Tbs. salt

cubed

2 c. red chili powder

2 gal. water

5 lbs. potatoes, peeled and

1/2 c. cornmeal

Cut meat into 1-inch cubes. Cover with water and bring to a boil. Reduce heat and simmer covered for about 4 hours. Add potatoes and salt. Cook for 1-1/2 hours.

Mix chili powder and cornmeal with enough water to make a thick paste. Stir paste slowly into stew. Simmer for 1/2 hour.

ACORN STEW

2 1/2 lbs. stew meat, cubed

2 large onions, diced

1 c. acorn meal

1 1/2 qt. water

Salt and pepper, to taste

Prepare acorn meal according to recipe located in Bread section. Place meat, onions, and water in stockpot. Bring to a boil then reduce heat. Simmer for 3-4 hours or until meat is tender. Add more water as necessary to have about 3 cups of broth. Add salt and pepper to taste. Remove meat and onions from pot. Set aside. To the broth, add acorn meal and stir well. Bring broth to a boil. Pour it over the meat mixture. Serve immediately.

CLAM CHOWDER

3 slices bacon

2 cans clams

2 Tbs. flour

6 potatoes, peeled and diced

1/8 tsp. pepper

2 yellow onions, minced

2 Tbs. butter

2 c. water

1 tsp. salt

Cut bacon into small strips and brown it. Add onions and sauté until golden. Drain clams and reserve liquid. Chop clams. Add clams to the pot with the onions. Mix in butter and flour. Heat, stirring for 2 minutes. Stir in clam juice and water. Add potatoes, salt, and pepper. Simmer, covered, for 2 hours, stirring occasionally.

PUEBLO POTATO-TOMATO SOUP

6 washed and cored tomatoes
and diced

8 medium potatoes, peeled

2 yellow onions, sliced

1 qt. water

1/2 small red chili pepper crushed
seeds

1 green pepper, sliced, include

1 tsp. fresh minced parsley

1 Tbs. salt

Place tomatoes, potatoes, onions, and water in large kettle. Simmer about 1 hour or until potatoes are tender. Mash potatoes slightly. Add chili pepper, green pepper, parsley, and salt. Simmer for 20 –25 minutes.

Panther in the Sky
The Story of Tecumseh
by Bill Talking Leaves Berdine

"Time rolls on without ceasing. Winter passes quickly away and the summer is here again. You shall soon glory in the strength of your manhood, and your enemies afar shall hear your name and tremble."
Methoataske, mother of Tecumtha

The man known among his followers as Shooting Star was born at Old Piqua, Ohio in 1768 to a Kispokotha Shawnee warrior chief and a Muscogee mother. It is said that Tecumseh claimed to have been born near what is now Clarksburg, WV. The translation of his name, Tecumtha or the more popular version, Tecumseh is "cougar crouching for his prey." It may have been nearer to Panther Passing in the Sky than Shooting Star, since according to at least one legend, that was the name given to the meteorite which appeared as he was being born.

Tenskwatawa, the Open Door (formerly Lalawethika, the Rattle) younger brother of Tecumseh, fell into a trance in 1805 from which he awoke with a vision of rejecting the white culture and ways and of uniting all Indians into a great confederacy to rise against the whites who had overrun the lands of the Shawnee and other Nations. It fell upon his brother, Tecumseh, to bring the vision into reality. He was, as was Tenskwatawa, dedicated to uniting all nations in eastern North America into one great nation.

The brothers in 1808 moved into Tippecanoe, a former Miami village in Indiana Territory to set up headquarters and to establish a place where

people from various nations could live free of the white ways and influence. The village which soon became known as Prophet's Town drew people from the Huron, Ojibwa, Potawatomi, Shawnee and other nations.
The U.S. had laid claim to what was then known as the Northwest Territory and Tecumseh left the village in charge of his brother with strict orders not to attack the whites under the leadership of W.H. Harrison, later president.

Harrison moved against the village with 1000 men claiming to be looking for stolen horses. Tenskwatawa was urged on by Winnebago militants and ordered an attack.

Tenskwatawa became the object of ridicule because the death of several of his warriors indicated that his strong medicine had become weakened. The allies deserted in droves.

Harrison attacked the vacated village and burned it, along with what weapons had been left behind.

Legend tells us that his vision of the great destruction caused by the Dec. 16, 1811 New Madrid (estimated 8.0) earthquake dramatically increased his stature among Native Americans who felt the jolts and jars as much as 1000 miles away. That one and the two quakes which followed created Reelfoot Lake in Tennessee and changed the course of the Mississippi and of history and left the residents sitting atop a split in their rift which could become active again tomorrow.

Tecumseh later joined the British in the War of 1812. They commissioned him as a Brigadier General. He is said to have predicted his death to almost the exact minute and just before the fatal battle, cast off his British general's uniform, dressed in deerskins for his impending death and led his warriors into the Battle of Thames at Chatham, Ontario.

He was killed on Oct. 5, 1813.

Gyantwakia

by Bill Talking Leaves Berdine

Don't let the Seneca phonetic spelling throw you. It has also been spelled Guyantwahia, Gyontwahia, Gyantawaky and perhaps as many as a dozen other ways not quite so common. That was a real problem with trying to spell something in a language which had no alphabet and no written version. Any Tom, Sean or Hans who came along spelled it the way it sounded to his ears and it often came out resembling Irish, English, Dutch or something else resembling one of those. Regardless of the way you see it written, it still means one of the great chiefs of the Seneca, Cornplanter.

There can be little doubt that Cornplanter spent some time in what is now West Virginia. The area around Salisbury in Somerset County in southern Pennsylvania near the present border with Maryland boasts of being the site of several villages of "Cornplanter Indians." Those villages have also been claimed to be the first settlements by Indians in that area. Salisbury can also boast today that it is only about 60 miles east of Morgantown. If you want to pick nits, make that Mt. Morris which is the first big city in PA after you head north out of Morgantown. Mt. Morris is what happened after my Granddaddy left his home in the elbow of the creek and made it hospitable for those who followed. My Seneca grandmother is buried on a hilltop just across the first knoll and outside the cemetery because she was Indian. I'm not giving you any better directions to the gravesite.

The Seneca Trail in West Virginia wasn't where most people today believe it was. Road signs have misled dozens of tourists who got tangled up in our hills and thought they were riding where Seneca moccasins had trod. They may have, but only if they strayed off the beaten path. The REAL Seneca Trail (it wasn't called that, you know) began on the Wapatomaka (my people called it that, which translates as "the place of the wild geese"). You probably know it better by its modern name, The South Branch of the Potomac. More and more people today are calling it by its ancient name, especially since my book came out reminding them of what it once was.

The trail crisscrossed the North Fork several times before heading up Seneca Creek and across the hilltops to what is now Shavers Fork and down that stream to a good footlog or shallow spot. I suspect (based on my own travels along said fork in search of rainbows) that crossing was a short distance above Parsons. A part of that trail then headed toward Elkins, not going back south or back east again, but WEST. They had already been south and east and Indians might have done some funny things and walked in some funny places, but not too many were so all-fired anxious to walk around in big circles. I suppose that much of the confusion has been caused by the fact there was a Mingo settlement on the north side of Cheat Mt. where 219 crosses today.

I suspect there was another branch of the trail which continued on down toward Parsons, crossed on the short way and headed toward the villages of the "Cornplanter Indians" in Somerset County, just east of the Youghiogheny. The villages were actually along the Casselman River, but I just wanted you to know that I could spell it although I haven't the foggiest notion of what it actually means. There is even a branch called "Indian Creek." And besides, everybody has heard of the Youghiogheny and who but Somersetters has ever heard of the Casselman? If you study a topo map, it is difficult to reach any other conclusion about the trails. Others agree that the so-called Seneca Trail enters the state near Parsons. Westbounders from those upper villages likely took the easy way out and strolled along the flat ground to rejoin the trail near what is now Kerens, but logic tells me that connector could not have been the main trail.

The main trail then went west along the Little Kanawha watershed to the Ohio and toward the major settlements along that river. It is almost one of those foregone conclusions that Chief Cornplanter, having taken credit for the villages east of the Youghiogheny and along the Casselman River, would have traveled to other outlying villages or settlements along the Wapatomaka and the Ohio.

That was a long way around to tell you that Chief Cornplanter was very likely in West Virginia before it was a gleam in the eye of Francis Pierpont.

Nobody knows for sure when Chief Cornplanter was born. It must have been after 1730 and before 1740. Many historians have settled on 1736 with a "c" in front. I'll go along with that, as long as they don't take away the "c".

There is just as much (and maybe more important) confusion about the name of his father. There is some agreement on the name, John O'Bail, but Daddy could have been a Scotsman, John O'Bain (changed to O'Bail to escape prosecution in England), or it could have been as others claim, a Dutchman by the name of Abeel. I like the first one better. And just to clear the fog, whatever his real moniker, he was married to Cornplanter's mother who was a daughter of the Seneca chief *gyusuthia.* Cornplanter was originally called *ganiodieu,* but later became "Cornplanter" because of the teasing by his playmates.

The Iroquois League was split during the American Revolution with Nations taking different sides. The Seneca and Cornplanter sided with the guys who wore the red targets and seemed to have the most people to shoot at. The choice was a disaster for the Senecas. One woman presented a dream to Council in which she described the devastation which *hanodaganears,* or "Town Destroyer", known to others as Washington, would wreak upon the people. The dream came all too true, but it was Sullivan who did the foul deeds at Washington's orders in 1779. The only real battle between Seneca (only) and Revolutionary forces in that area took place at Kashong Creek. That campaign, led by General John Sullivan, resulted in the total destruction of more than 40 villages, an estimated 150,000 bushels of corn and untold numbers of dead from battle and the ensuing starvation. I hope you noticed the amount of corn. That alone should put the lie to the claim that Indians were not at all numerous.

Cornplanter was beaten. He signed a treaty and ceded a great deal of land to the United States. That treaty and his continuing friendship for whites placed him in disfavor with his people. Cornplanter became friendly toward the United States following the war and was later acquainted with Washington, Jefferson and others in the new government. He received a number of gifts from various officials.

Cornplanter was deposed as Chief and his bitter adversary, *otetiani,* "always ready" or Red Jacket, replaced him. Red Jacket's name became *sagoyewatha* or "keeper awake" and Cornplanter became *onono* or "cold one."

Cornplanter, at some later date, had a dream. He approached several people for an interpretation and eventually found a man who interpreted it to mean that he should destroy all the great number of gifts he had received from the whites. He acknowledged this as the true meaning of his dream and burned everything but his valued tomahawk. He was also told that his service to the Nation was over and that he should step down. This was supposed to have occurred about 1810. I have heard the story of the dream only once several years ago and have not seen it confirmed.

CORNPLANTER DIED ON FEB. 18, 1836 AT THE ESTIMATED AGE OF 100.

BREADS

BAKING BREAD

To bake bread while traveling, pieces of chestnut bark were cut from trees. Bread batter, such as for traditional cornbread, was placed inside the fresh bark and this was set close to the fire to bake. The bread was flavored by the bark and the moisture in the bark kept the bread from becoming too dry.

BREAD _By Bill Talking Leaves Berdine_

The Cherokee word for bread is "ga du." There were many types of bread. Most was originally made from cornmeal and included such items as salt rising, walnut, chestnut, cracklin's, ash cakes, corn dodgers, pone and hoecakes. The widespread use of wheat flour for bread came later, after the arrival of the Europeans. The Europeans' "corn" was really oats before they came to this country and learned about the Indians' maize. The Scottish word, "cornt" then meant "fed oats." It still does.

CHIPPEWA BANNOCK

1 1/2 c. cornmeal
1/2 c. water
4 Tbs. hazelnut oil, melted butter or bacon drippings
4 Tbs. maple syrup or honey
1/2 tsp. salt (optional)
3 - 4 Tbs. cooking oil, for frying

In a mixing bowl, combine cornmeal, water, hazelnut oil, syrup, and salt (if used). In large skillet, heat 2 tablespoons oil over medium heat. Drop cakes by tablespoonful into skillet and flatten with back of spoon. Fry cakes until crisp and brown on both sides. Add more oil to skillet as needed.

CHESTNUT CAKES

1 lb. chestnuts, roasted
Cornmeal
Oil for frying

1/2 small onion, chopped fine
Boiling water
Salt

Cool roasted chestnuts and peel. Puree chestnuts. Add onion and enough cornmeal and water to make thick dough. Shape hamburger-sized patties. Fry in hot oil until golden on each side. Drain, salt, and eat.
NOTE: Do not add salt before cooking. It causes cornmeal mixture to crumble.

CHEROKEE BEAN BREAD

2 c. dried beans, soaked overnight and then cooked to tenderness
4 c. cornmeal
1/2 c. wheat flour
1 tsp. baking soda
Milk to make batter (optional)
1-3 Tbs. sugar, to taste (optional)
Melted butter, margarine or bacon grease

Remove the beans from the soup and mash the beans fine. Use the soup from the beans to moisten the cornmeal. Mix in the mashed bean pulp and sugar. Stir until well mixed and uniform. Add more soup to get a good consistency for pouring and baking. (Depending on how fine you mashed the beans there will probably still be chunks of bean visible.) Pour into a greased pan and bake at 400-425° F. until the top of the bread is light brown. Remove from the oven and cool on a wire rack.   Brush the top with melted butter, margarine, or bacon grease.

NOTE: This was a traditional bread that was a favorite of both the Cherokee and also the European settlers because it was tasty and kept well for several days. Don't overcook! This bread tends to brown on the bottom first. A cast iron skillet is perfect for this but modern glass or ceramic casseroles also work well. This bread tends to be a little easier to cut into pieces compared to regular corn bread but can still be crumbly if not cooked just right. This bread can be wrapped in foil or plastic wrap (leather in the old days) and carried on the trail for a high protein snack or meal. Some folks like to use Milk instead of the bean soup to make the batter. This makes a much sweeter bean bread with less bean flavor. Another traditional way to cook this bread is to make the mixture slightly more firm and drop in boiling water to cook like dumplings for 30 minutes. The dumplings cooked this way should be served at the next meal and don't keep as well as the oven or pan-cooked version.

CHESTNUT BREAD

Peel chestnuts. Remove skins. Pound. Add cornmeal and some water. Make into small balls. Wrap in green corn husks and tie tightly. Cook in boiling water until done.

CORNBREAD

2 c. cornmeal   Cold water to make stiff
dough

Working well with both hands, pat out size desired. Bake quickly over hot coals or in hot iron skillet.

CRANBERRY CORNBREAD

1 c. unbleached flour   1 1/3 c. yellow cornmeal
1 Tbs. baking powder   1/2 tsp. salt
1/2 c. dried cranberries   2 large eggs
1/4 c. honey   1 c. milk
2 Tbs. sunflower oil   Cooking spray

Preheat oven to 400° and lightly spray an 8-inch-square baking pan. In a mixing bowl, whisk together flour, cornmeal, baking powder and salt. Stir in cranberries and set aside. In another bowl, whisk together eggs, milk, honey, and oil. Add to dry ingredients and mix just until blended. Pour batter into prepared pan and bake until the top is lightly browned and a toothpick inserted in the center comes out clean, approximately 30 minutes.

MAMAW PARKINS' CORNBREAD

1 c. cornmeal

1 scoop (1/2 c.) oats

1 egg

2 Tbs. sugar

1 c. wheat flour

1 scoop (1/2 c.) potato flakes

1 tsp. baking soda

1 1/4 c. buttermilk

Lightly oil a large skillet and heat in oven to 375°. Mix cornmeal and other ingredients without dallying and bake until golden brown.

BOB EAGLECLAW PARKINS

BLUE CORN TORTILLAS

Tortillas can be made by mixing blue cornmeal with salt and water. Pat the dough into thin sheets between your palms. Brown quickly on both sides on a hot griddle.

FLAT DUMPLINGS

3 c. cornmeal

1/2 c. ash lye

1 tsp. salt

Boiling water

Mix cornmeal, salt, and lye together. Pour boiling water over mixture to make a stiff dough. Make dumplings flat. Boil in water until done. After cooling, split open and spread in a flat basket. Pass basket over flames four times, once to the North, East, South, and West. Set basket outside to freeze. Eat in the morning while still frozen.

NOTE: Ash lye can be replaced by 1 tsp. soda. Obviously, this is a winter food.

HOE CAKES

2 c. water

2 tsp. salt

2 c. cornmeal

2 Tbs. butter

1 Tbs. fresh dill, chopped (optional)

Preheat oven to 375° F. Bring water to boil in a saucepan. Add cornmeal, salt, butter, and dill (if used). Pour into buttered 8x8-inch cake pan and bake for approximately 25 minutes. Cut into squares and serve.

HOECAKES

2 c. yellow cornmeal (white will work, but I prefer yellow)
1/2 tsp. salt
Mix dry ingredients.
1 c. hot water   1 1/2 c. cold water
2 Tbs. melted fat (bacon grease or equivalent of other shortening)
Place dry mix in large bowl and add hot water to form a thick batter. Add only enough cold water to thin so that it will pour slowly. Add fat. Stir. Drop spoonfuls of batter onto hot skillet. Brown both sides. Best served hot.

Little Flower and Talking Leaves

CRACKLIN' BREAD

Use dough recipe given for Hoecakes above.
Make cracklin's by rendering bacon skins until they are quite crisp. Break into very small pieces, using enough to make a full cup. Add only enough hot water to dry mix so that it makes a thick dough which can be shaped into fairly small loaves. Add cracklins to dough and mix thoroughly by hand kneading. Bake at 400-450° F. for about 45 minutes. Best served hot with butter. Add jam or jelly for your sweet tooth.

Little Flower and Talking Leaves

CORN DODGERS

Use the same dough recipe as for the Hoecakes, adding only enough hot water to make a thick dough. Form into small balls about 1 1/2 -inches in diameter (I would have told you, "A little bigger than a golf ball", but Indians weren't silly enough to play golf.) Carefully, drop or spoon balls into deep HOT fat and fry until hard crust forms.

NOTE: These could be carried by the dozen in a pouch or shirttail while trekking through the underbrush in search of something better to eat. They were eaten either hot or cold. On the trail, six dodgers and a big swig of branch water would make you feel as though you had eaten a full meal.

Little Flower and Talking Leaves

SOFT BREAD

1 3/4 c. water
3/4 tsp. salt
Sunflower seeds

2/3 c. white cornmeal
Margarine or shortening

Bring the water to a boil. Mix together the cornmeal and salt. Pour the boiling water onto the dry ingredients while stirring. Continue to stir until the mixture become thick and smooth. Serve topped with margarine and sunflower seeds.

OLD-FASHIONED CORN PONE

6 c. cornmeal (country meal)
1 c. dry meal
1/2 c. flour
1 tsp. soda
1 tsp. baking powder

2 eggs
1/2 c. buttermilk
1 tsp. salt
1/4 c. oil
1/2 c. sugar

Scald the 6 cups country meal just enough to have meal wet and chunky. Add other cup of meal and 1/2 c. flour. Stir in just enough warm water to make a soft dough (not too much). As it sweetens, it gets thin. Set in warm place overnight. It bubbles or foams, has a peculiar odor when it is ready to add other ingredients. Beat eggs, add soda to buttermilk. Add eggs, soda and buttermilk, salt, oil, baking powder and sugar. Beat all of these together with first mixture which as set overnight. Grease pans. This recipe makes a large corn pone (or 2 loaf pans.) Bake at 450° F. for 1 hour and 20 minutes.

FRIED SQUASH BREAD

Wash, clean, and dice 2 summer squash and cook until soft. Do not cook dry. Leave about 3/4 cup of water in pot.

Combine: 1 c. cornmeal or cornmeal mix
1 egg
1/3 c. buttermilk

Add squash and water and mix together. Fry in hot oil until golden brown.

MIWOK BISCUITS

Make dough from acorn meal and water. Roll into balls, flatten. Bake on top of very hot rock. To make acorn meal: Grind acorns between rocks. Fan acorns with a fanning basket. (The fine particles will stick to the basket.) Put fine meal into a wooden bin. Pour warm water over it 3-4 times to take out bitter taste.

Dot Vurnovas

HOLE BREAD

1 c. self-rising flour
1 pinch salt
1/4 c. water
Prepare a 1-foot deep hole near fire to which 2 shovel-fulls of hot coals and ash have been added. Grease aluminum foil and wrap loosely around dough. Put wrapped dough in hole. Dough will increase by 1/3 or 1/2 volume during baking. If the temperature is too hot, the outside of the bread will be black; if it is too cool, the inside will be elastic.

INDIAN FIELD BREAD

Heat approximately 5 cups oil in small pot.
Mix:

1 c. self-rising flour	1 tsp. baking powder
1/2 tsp. cinnamon	Pinch of salt
1 Tbs. oil	Enough milk to mix

Drop by spoonful into hot oil. Cook until brown and crisp, turning in oil. Put on paper towel to drain. Sprinkle with powdered sugar when cool or drizzle with hot-cake syrup.

Charless Falk Many Tears

FRIED TOMATO PONES

2 c. peeled, seeded tomatoes   Salt & pepper, to taste
1 c. cornmeal   1/4 c. sliced green onions (optional)
Bacon drippings

Place tomatoes and onions in mixing bowl. Add salt and pepper, to taste.
Add enough cornmeal to form pones or patties. Heat bacon drippings in
large skillet over medium heat. Fry pones for 2-3 minutes on each side
until golden brown. Serve hot.

SWEET POTATO BREAD

1 large can sweet potatoes in light syrup or 2 large raw sweet potatoes
2 c. cornmeal
1 tsp. soda
1/2 to 1 c. milk (optional)

Cook raw sweet potatoes until done.   Sweet potatoes can be boiled or
baked. If you are using canned sweet potatoes or are boiling the sweet
potatoes, peel the skins before boiling, and cook until sweet potatoes are
soft. Remove the potatoes from the syrup and save the syrup to make the
batter. If you are baking the sweet potatoes, cook them until the pulp is
soft and then remove the pulp from the skins. Discard the skins.   If you
use canned sweet potatoes in heavy syrup you may want to discard some of
the syrup or the resulting bread may be too sweet.
Mash the sweet potato pulp fine. Use some of the light syrup from the
potatoes to moisten the cornmeal then blend in the mashed sweet
potatoes. Use the milk or the additional syrup if necessary and blend to
the normal consistency for cornmeal batter. Pour batter into a greased
skillet or baking dish and bake until lightly browned and a toothpick stuck
into the bread comes out clean.
NOTE: This is a very tasty bread which can also be served as a dessert.
Some children will eat 5-6 pieces if the adults aren't watching. Sweet
Potato Bread is similar to Bean Bread in being a flavorful cornbread. It
keeps well but is so tasty it rarely lasts beyond the next meal.

CATTAIL FLOUR

Peel roots while wet. Then dry the roots. Chop into small pieces and pound into flour. Remove long fibers as they appear.

NOTE: Peeled cattails are delicious vegetables; the tops and stems, when young, can be steamed or boiled and eaten.

INTERTRIBAL BREAD

3 c. flour

2 1/2 tsp. baking powder or wood ash

1 Tbs. sugar

Water, lukewarm

2 Tbs. lard or bear fat

Mix all ingredients with enough lukewarm water to make thick dough. Knead well. Divide into 2 parts. On floured board, roll to about 1-inch thickness. Bake on greased pan at 375° F. until done. Makes 2 loaves.

NAVAJO BLUE CORN PANCAKES

1 c. blue cornmeal

1 tsp. baking powder

1 c. milk

1 tsp. baking soda

1 Tbs. sugar

1 tsp. salt

1 Tbs. melted butter

2 eggs, beaten

Honey or syrup for topping

Combine and mix dry ingredients. Add butter, eggs, milk, and stir well. Let batter sit for a few minutes. Spoon batter onto a medium-hot oiled skillet. Cook until lightly browned or about 2 minutes on each side. Serve with honey or syrup.

FRY BREAD

1 lb. 6 oz. flour
1 lb. lard to fry bread
1 1/4 tsp. salt
1/2-inch bits
1 3/4 c. ice water
rosemary

6 oz. dry milk
3/4 oz. baking powder
2 1/2 oz. lard, cut into

1 Tbs. minced
1 Tbs. minced thyme

Combine flour, milk, baking powder, and salt. Sift into large bowl. Add lard, thyme, and rosemary. Rub together until mixture resembles coarse meal. Pour in water. Gather into ball. Cover bowl and let dough rest at room temperature for 2 hours. Roll dough out until 1/2-inch thick. Cut three circles out of dough, about 6-1/2 inches in diameter. Cut two parallel slits completely through dough, down the center of each round, spacing the slits about 1 inch apart. Melt lard in a large cast iron skillet. Heat until hot, but not smoking. Fry rounds one at a time, cooking about 2 minutes on each side until golden brown. Drain bread on paper towels. Makes 3 loaves.

BLACKFEET FRY BREAD

4 c. flour
1 Tbs. baking powder
1 1/2 c. warm water

1 Tbs. powdered milk
1 tsp. salt
Oil for frying

Mix all dry ingredients thoroughly. Add water. Knead until soft, then set aside for 1 hour. Shape into small balls. Flatten each ball into a circle with rolling pin or by hand. Fry in a skillet half-full of oil until golden brown on both sides.

DEBBIE'S FRY BREAD

3 c. unbleached flour   1 Tbs. baking powder
1 tsp. salt
Put all ingredients in bowl and whisk.
Add 1-1/2 cups water or warm milk to mixture and stir.
Add 1 Tbs. vegetable oil

Knead gently to form dough into ball. Cover and let rise in warm place 30 minutes. Roll out on flour-covered board.

Fry in hot oil in iron skillet about 1 minute on each side.

Debra Bostic

DI-GA-NU-LI (DOGHEADS)

Grit roasting ear corn after it gets too hard for roasting ears. The meal will be as hard as soft mush. Find green corn shucks and wash them. Pat out corn dough to fit shucks. Put dough on widest end of shuck. Double the shuck back over the dough 5 or 6 inches, then pull shuck around the dough. Tie and put in a kettle of boiling water. Boil until done. Serve hot with butter.

NAVAJO FRY BREAD

3 c. unbleached flour, sifted   1/2 c. dry powdered milk
1 Tbs. baking powder   1/2 tsp. salt
1/2 c. warm water or milk   2 qts. oil for deep frying

Combine the first 5 ingredients in a large mixing bowl and knead until smooth and soft, but not sticky. Depending on the altitude and humidity, you may need to adjust the liquid or the flour, so go slowly and balance accordingly. Be careful not to overwork the dough, or it will become tough and chewy. Brush a tablespoon of oil over the finished dough and allow it to rest 20 minutes to 2 hours in a bowl covered with a damp cloth. After the dough has rested, heat the oil in a broad deep frying pan or kettle until it reaches a low boil (375°). Pull off egg-sized balls of dough and quickly roll, pull, and pat them out into large plate-sized rounds. They should be thin in the middle and about $\frac{1}{4}$-inch thick at the edges. Carefully ease each piece of flattened dough into the hot, boiling oil, one at a time. Using a long-handled cooking fork or tongs, turn the dough one time. Allow about 2 minutes cooking time per side. When golden brown, lift from oil, shake gently to remove bulk of oil, and place on layered brown paper or paper towels to finish draining. Serve hot with honey, jelly, fine powdered sugar, or various meat toppings.

Hint: The magic is in frying the bread quickly! The hotter the oil, the less time it takes to cook. The less time it takes to cook, the lighter the texture and lower the fat content.

PUMPKIN BREAD

1 1/2 c. flour   1 1/2 c. puréed cooked pumpkin
3/4 c. sugar   2 eggs
1/2 c. melted butter   1/2 tsp. nutmeg
1 tsp. baking powder   1/2 tsp. salt
1/4 tsp. cloves   1/2 c. raisins
1/3 c. milk   1/2 c. nuts

Preheat oven to 350°. Combine and mix together flour, sugar, baking powder, spices, and salt. Add pumpkin, butter, eggs, and milk, mixing well. Add nuts and raisins. Pour batter into a greased 6" x 9" loaf pan. Bake 1 hour, or until a knife inserted into loaf comes out clean.

PUMPKIN PINE NUT BREAD

1 1/2 c. self-rising flour pumpkin
3/4 c. sugar
1/2 c. butter, melted
1 tsp. cinnamon
1/2 tsp. allspice

1 c. mashed or pureed cooked
2 eggs, beaten
1 tsp. nutmeg
2 Tbs. vanilla
3/4 c. pine nuts

Preheat oven to 350°. In a mixing bowl, combine flour, pumpkin, sugar, butter, eggs, cinnamon, nutmeg, allspice, and vanilla. Stir in pine nuts. Place batter in a greased 6" x 9" bread pan. Bake 1 hour, or until a knife inserted in bread comes out clean. Makes 1 loaf.

William D. Stone (Waya)

PAW PAW PONES

2 c. cornmeal
1 to 2 c. paw paw pulp
1 3-finger pinch wood ashes or 1 quick sprinkle of salt from large shaker
1 tsp. baking powder
1 c. dried currants, raisins, blackberries, or strawberries*
Nutmeg or allspice, to taste

Mix together. If more moisture is needed, use more paw paw pulp or water. Too much paw paw can be overpowering. Dollop by full Tablespoon onto cookie sheet. Bake at 375° for 12-18 minutes. Be careful not to burn the bottoms.

Note: It is important to use dried berries for texture and taste. Reconstitute berries in warm water for 1/2 hour. They should still have some "chew" in them.

Dark Rain Thom

ZUNI BREAD

7/8 c. buttermilk	2 egg whites
2 c. whole wheat flour	1 c. bread flour
1/3 c. cornmeal	2 Tbs. applesauce
3 Tbs. molasses	1/2 c. dry roasted sunflower
seeds	
1/4 tsp. baking soda	3 tsp. yeast

Mix all ingredients into a dough and let rise. Form into a flat round loaf about 1 inch thick. Bake at 350° until golden brown.

CORN FRITTERS

Mix:	1 c. flour	1 1/2 tsp. baking powder
	2 Tbs. sugar	1/4 tsp. salt

Add: 1 whole egg to 1/2 cup milk. Blend these thoroughly.

Gradually add dry ingredients to liquid, stirring well.

Add 1 can drained whole kernel golden corn to the mixture. Stir until corn is distributed throughout batter. May be dropped on a hot skillet by large spoonfuls to make fritters 2 to 3 inches in diameter and the thickness of pancakes. Fry in greased hot skillet or in deep fat until golden brown. If you use deep fat, it should be hot enough to brown a cube of bread in 1 minute. Do not overload the skillet. Serve hot with butter and syrup or jam. The batter may be used for other fruit or vegetables, raw or cooked. If raw materials are used, allow to cook through.

Talking Leaves and Little Flower

ACORN MEAL

Pound shelled acorns. Place in cotton bag, and submerge in running water for a few days. Shake occasionally to wash out tannins. Remove, drain, and spread in sun to dry.

CHEROKEE CORN PONES

2 c. cornmeal
1 tsp. salt
3/4 c. buttermilk
Butter

1/4 tsp. baking soda
1/2 c. shortening
3/4 c. milk

Combine cornmeal, baking soda, and salt; cut in shortening until mixture resembles coarse meal. Add buttermilk and milk, stirring just until dry ingredients are moistened. Form batter into eight 1/2-inch thick cakes. Place on a hot, greased griddle. Bake at 400° for 15 minutes. Turn and bake and additional 15 minutes. Serve hot with butter. Serves 8.

CHEROKEE HUCKLEBERRY BREAD

2 c. self-rising flour
1 c. sugar
1 c. milk
2 c. huckleberries

1 egg
1 stick butter
1 tsp. vanilla extract

Cream eggs, butter, and sugar together. Add flour, milk, and vanilla. Sprinkle flour on berries to prevent them from going to the bottom. Add berries to mixture. Put in baking pan and bake at 350° F. for approximately 40 minutes or until down.

NOTE: Blueberries can be used to replace huckleberries.

BLUEBERRY BREAD

3 c. all-purpose flour
1 1/2 tsp. salt
1 c. blueberries

1 Tbs. baking powder
1 1/2 c. water

Mix flour, baking powder, and salt. Add water quickly and stir. Add blueberries into batter. Spread batter in an 8"x8"x2" baking pan. Bake at 425° F. for 20 minutes. Can be served hot or cold.

CHEROKEE SWEET BREAD

Flour
Baking soda
Baking powder
Molasses, sugar or honey

Make a dough from flour as if you were going to make biscuits. Add some molasses, sugar, or honey. Bake this in small or large pones, whichever you prefer. Eat it as you would any cake.

SWEET BISCUITS

1 c. shortening
1 c. sugar
dough
1/2 c. molasses
2 eggs
1 tsp. soda

1 tsp. baking powder
Enough flour to make stiff

1 1/2 tsp. ginger
1 tsp. vanilla extract

Sift together dry ingredients. Cut shortening into mixture until it resembles coarse meal. Add molasses, eggs, and vanilla extract. Knead until a stiff consistency is achieved. Roll into thin layer. Cut with biscuit cutter or a glass. Bake at 400° F. until golden brown.

Melissie Landreth

BLUE CORN SCONES

1/2 c. blue cornmeal
1/3 tsp. baking powder
1/4 lb. chilled butter
1 egg
1/2 tsp. vanilla extract

1 3/4 c. all-purpose flour
1/4 tsp. salt
1/4 c. light brown sugar
1/2 c. milk

Preheat oven to 375° F. Grease and flour baking sheet. Stir the dry ingredients in a bowl, then cut the butter into the dry mixture to form a coarse meal. Beat the egg with milk, sugar, and vanilla. When smooth, stir into the dry mixture until the dough holds together. Knead briefly on a floured surface. Pat into an 8" circle. Place on baking sheet. With a pizza cutter or serrated knife, score circle into 8 wedges. Bake for 15 to 10 minutes or until nicely brown. Serve with honey, fruits, or jam.

ZUNI FEAST DAY BREAD PUFFS

2 c. all-purpose flour (or 1 1/2 c. all-purpose + 1/2 c. tepary bean flour)
2 Tbs. baking powder
1/2 tsp. salt
1 whole green onion, diced fine
1/2 c. cilantro, diced fine
1/4 tsp. ground pepper
1/4 tsp. chili powder
1/4 tsp. thyme
1/4 tsp. cumin
1 c. cold water or milk
2 tsp. honey
Oil for frying

In a large, deep bowl, mix all dry and fresh ingredients. Make a well in the center and add the cold water or milk and the honey. Stir dough until all ingredients are thoroughly blended. Dough should be sticky. Heat about 1 inch of oil in a deep frying pan to about 375° F. and just bubbling. Carefully drop dough by generous tablespoonfuls into the hot oil, two or three pieces at a time. Fry quickly, turning so that all surfaces become light golden-honey colored. Drain on layers of clean brown paper or paper towels. Serve quickly.

SUNFLOWER SEED BREAD

3 1/4 c sunflower seeds
2 1/2 tsp. salt
2/3 c. oil for frying

3 1/4 c. water
6 Tbs. cornmeal

Put sunflower seeds, water, and salt into a pot. Cover and simmer for 1 1/2 hours until well cooked. Crush the seeds into a paste. Add cornmeal, 1 Tbs. at a time to thicken. Knead dough. Make small, flat cakes approximately 5" in diameter. Heat oil and fry both sides, adding more oil if necessary. Drain well.

WILD SAGE BREAD

1 pkg. yeast

1 c. cottage cheese

1 Tbs. melted shortening

2 tsp. crushed dried sage

1/4 tsp. baking soda

1 Tbs. roasted pine nuts, crushed

1/4 c. warm water

1 egg

1 Tbs. sugar

1/2 tsp. salt

2 1/2 c. flour

Combine sugar, sage, salt, baking soda, and flour. Dissolve yeast in 1/4 c. warm water. Beat egg and cottage cheese together until smooth. Add melted shortening and yeast. Add flour mixture slowly to egg mixture, beating well after each addition until a stiff dough is formed. Cover dough with cloth and put in warm place to raise until doubled (about 1 hour). Punch down dough, knead for 1 minute, and place in well-greased loaf pan. Cover and let rise for 40 minutes. Bake at 350° F. for 50 minutes. Brush top with melted shortening and sprinkle with crushed, roasted pine nuts.

CHEYENNE BATTER BREAD

1 qt. milk

2 c. white cornmeal

3 eggs, separated

1 Tbs. butter, melted

1/2 tsp. salt

Bring milk to a full boil. Slowly stir in cornmeal. Cool mixture. Add well-beaten egg yolks, melted butter, and salt. Add stiffly beaten egg whites. Bake at 375° F. until done.

WILD RICE PANCAKES

2 c. wild rice, cooked and cooled

3/4 c. chopped green onions

Sunflower oil

about 2 eggs, beaten

Salt and pepper, to taste

Mix rice, onions, and eggs. Heat oil that is about 1/4" deep in skillet. When oil is hot, add mixture to make 3" pancakes. Flatten cakes into oil and turn when edges are browned. Drain on brown paper or paper towels.

NOTE: Add only enough egg to bind mixture. Too much makes a rice omelet.

BREAD-ON-A-STICK

Easy way:

2 c. Bisquick® or other biscuit mix   1/2 c. water

Mix thoroughly. It may be necessary to add more mix in order to make a dough thick enough to stay on the stick.

Cut a green limb about 1 1/2" in diameter and 3' long from an oak, American hornbeam, sassafras, beech, birch, or other tree that will not give bread a bad flavor. Remove bark for at least 10" from upper end. Sharpen lower end and insert into ground so that peeled end is about 15" above fire. Wrap dough about 3/4" thick around peeled portion and bake slowly, turning occasionally until heavy brown crust is formed. Don't eat the splinters.

Hard way: (from scratch)

2 c. white flour   1/2 c. water
1/2 tsp. salt   3 tsp. baking powder
2 Tbs. shortening

Mix together the dry ingredients. Work in shortening, mixing thoroughly. Add only enough water (or milk), mixing slowly, until the dough is thick enough to stay on the stick.

NOTE: It is a good idea to prepare your dry mix at home and carry it with you in a plastic bag. We Indians are smart enough to take advantage of all the new-fangled supplies that our forefathers lacked.

Bill Talking Leaves Berdine

YELLOW CORNMEAL DUMPLINGS

1 c. yellow cornmeal   1 c. all-purpose flour
2 tsp. baking powder   2 tsp. dry dill
1 tsp. salt   1/4 tsp. pepper
1/4 c. water   1 Tbs. olive oil
2 eggs

Combine cornmeal, flour, baking powder, dill, salt, and pepper in a medium bowl. Combine water, olive oil, and eggs separately, stirring well. Add to cornmeal mixture. Blend well. With moistened hands, shape dough into 1-inch balls and set aside. Bring 2 quarts water to a simmer in a large saucepan and add 1/2 of the dumplings. Cover and cook without letting water boil for 10 minutes or until done. Remove with a slotted spoon. Set cooked dumplings aside, but keep them warm while cooking the remaining dumplings. Serve with soup or stew.

PUMPKIN MUFFINS

1 c. raisins
2 eggs
1/2 c. sugar
1/2 tsp. cinnamon
1/3 c. canola oil
3/4 c. whole wheat flour
1/2 tsp. baking soda

1/2 c. orange juice
1 c. canned or cooked pumpkin
1/2 tsp. cloves
1/2 tsp. salt
1 c. all-purpose flour
1-1/2 tsp. baking powder

Soak raising in orange juice for 5 minutes. Do not drain. In large bowl, stir in pumpkin, eggs, sugar, cloves, cinnamon, and salt. Add oil, mixing well. Stir together flours, baking powder and baking soda. Add to pumpkin mixture with the raisin-orange juice mixture and stir well. Fill paper-lined muffin cups 2/3 full. Bake at 400° F. for about 25 minutes or until done.

HONEY FLAT BREAD

1 c. flour
Cinnamon, to taste

1/4 c. water
Honey, to taste

Mix flour and water. Stir in cinnamon and honey. Pour into a small, greased baking pan and bake at 325° F. until done.

MOHAWK CORNBREAD

2 lbs. corn flour

2 16-oz. cans kidney beans, drained

Salt, to taste

Water

Mix flour, salt, beans and water to form stiff dough. Form into flattened cakes about 6 inches in diameter and 2 inches thick. Drop carefully into a kettle of boiling water. Cover and boil for about 1 hour. Lift out of kettle and serve with butter.

CORNBREAD SAGE DRESSING

Cornbread

4 ribs celery, diced

4 Tbs. poultry seasoning

Turkey stock

3 Tbs. oil

1 large yellow onion, diced

4 Tbs. minced fresh sage

Prepare cornbread according to your favorite recipe. Allow it to cool thoroughly and crumble into a large bowl. Set aside. Preheat oven to 325° F. Prepare baking dish by spraying with vegetable oil. Heat oil in medium saucepan over medium heat. Sauté celery and onion with poultry seasoning and sage until onion becomes translucent. Add onion mixture to crumbled cornbread and mix well. Add enough turkey stock to moisten dressing well. Spoon into baking dish and bake 20-30 minutes.

NOTE: One of my favorite additions to this dressing is 1/2 cup pecans or English walnuts, coarsely chopped.

Maka (Connie Stone)

CORN FINGERS

1 c. yellow cornmeal

1/4 c. grated Monterey jack cheese

4 c. water

1 1/2 Tbs. salt

1/4 c. soft butter

Bring water and salt to a boil. Slowly add cornmeal, stirring constantly. Cook for 20 minutes. Turn into a buttered 8-inch square pan and chill until firm. Cut firm cornmeal mixture into strips 1-inch X 2-inches. Split each strip in half. Spread with butter and sprinkle on cheese. Put halves together and sprinkle again with cheese. Place on a buttered baking sheet and bake at 400° F. for 15 minutes or until brown.

BUTTERMILK BISCUITS

2 c. all-purpose flour   1 Tbs. baking powder
3/4 tsp. salt   1/2 tsp. baking soda
5 Tbs. chilled vegetable shortening   1 c. buttermilk

Preheat oven to 425° F. In a large bowl, sift together flour, baking soda, baking powder, and salt. Cut shortening into flour mixture, using a pastry blender or 2 butter knives. Mixture should form coarse crumbs. Add buttermilk, blending with a fork until dough holds together. Turn dough
 onto a floured surface and form into a disk. Knead lightly just a few times until smooth. Pat dough to a 3/4-inch thickness. Using a biscuit cutter or glass dipped in flour, cut out biscuits. Place biscuits about 2 inches apart on a ungreased baking sheet. Gather the trimmings and repeat forming and cutting. Bake 12 – 15 minutes or until golden brown.

Hazel Lodmell

CORN CAKE

1 c. pounded corn   1/3 c. water
Cinnamon   Honey
Butter to fry

Pound hard corn until powder-like. Pour in water. Sprinkle in cinnamon. Add a small amount of honey. Form mixture into a rounded cake. Place in melted butter and fry, flipping occasionally to ensure cake is thoroughly cooked. It should be golden brown.

BLUEBERRY FRITTERS

18 oz. frozen blueberries
3/4 c. sugar
3 c. oil for frying

4 c. flour
3 1/2 tsp. baking powder
5 eggs

Thaw blueberries and reserve liquid. Sift together dry ingredients. Measure the blueberry liquid. If necessary, add water to make 1/2 cup. Heat oil to 350° F. in deep fryer. Beat eggs with blueberry liquid until foamy. Mix into dry ingredients and fold in berries. Drop from a tablespoon into hot oil. Turn fritter frequently so they become chocolate brown on all sides. Drain on paper towels. Serve hot.

MOM'S CORNBREAD

1 1/4 c. flour
Meal®
1/2 c. sugar
1/2 tsp. salt
2 eggs

3/4 c. yellow Quaker Corn

1/2 c. oil
1 c. milk
2 tsp. baking powder

Combine dry ingredients together. Whip eggs than add to dry ingredients. Add oil and mix. Add milk last and mix. Place in Pam®-sprayed or oiled pan. Bake for 25 minutes at 425° F. oven.

Sharon Elizabeth Martin shared this recipe created by her mother, Mary Evelyn Garrett

Night Walker

As we walk through the darkness, the moon sometimes shines bold and lights
our way.
It is other times cloudy and we have a difficult time picking our path in the
dark, black night.

We listen to the sound of reverberating silence, close our eyes,
And take a deep breath of the damp air.

All the while we think that we are alone in the darkness.

Do we cry out for help, or should we trudge on alone, wandering aimlessly in
no set direction?

Do we allow fear to envelope our senses, or do we use fear for out faith to
come alive, Giving us confident strength?

The stars begin to shine as the clouds start to clear, and we stare in awe of
 their infinite number
And marvel at their beauty.
We hear an owl hoot and a coyote howl off in the distance.
It is here we realize we are never alone.
He who made all, loves all.
It is we, who choose to walk alone, without faith.
He who gave birth to the moon provides us with the light to see the better
 path.
It is up to us to be strong in times of fear and doubt.
"Faith the size of a mustard seed can move mountains."

With this, we can be like the hunting owl, who is undaunted by the darkness
And knows what is, is.
We may never fully understand what is, and what is going to be,
But let us be like the owl and be aware of the important things that we need
to survive in the night.
"Yea, though I walk through the valley of the shadow of death, I will fear
no evil: for thou art with me;
thy rod and they staff they comfort me." Aho.

Joshua Grey Fox Caldwell

Will Thomas

Did the Cherokee ever have a White Chief?

Many would respond, "No way that would never happen." When we look at Cherokee history, we find that there was a white chief of the Cherokee.

William Holland Thomas was a white Cherokee Chief. Will Thomas was born in 1805 on Raccoon Creek neat Waynesville, North Carolina. When he reached the age of 12, he was working for Felix Walker at a trading post on Soco Creek. He learned the Cherokee language during his work here. Drowning Bear, the Chief of Quallatown, learned that Will had no father, brothers, or sisters, and he took a special interest in him. He adopted Will as his son when he was 13 years old. Will's best friend, a Cherokee boy, taught him the ancient customs, lore and religious rites. Walker went broke and he gave Thomas what was left of the stock and some old law books. Through Will's own efforts, he studied the law books and gained the law knowledge that allowed him to become the legal representative for the Eastern Band of the Cherokee.

At the time the Cherokee gave up more land on the upper Little Tennessee River, he settled his mother on a farm on the Oconaluftee River. At the time of removal, he had prospered and owned 5 trading posts in the Cherokee Nation. During the forced removal, he assisted in tracking down the Cherokee. The motive for this was to help the Quallatown Cherokees to stay in North Carolina. Following Tsali's death, Thomas went to Washington to work out legal arrangements that would allow the Quallatown Cherokees to stay in North Carolina. Drowning Bear passed the position of Chief to Will Thomas as his adopted father. In 1840, Thomas was appointed to act as the government's disbursing agent. Will used the money to begin to purchase of more then 50,000 acres of land for the Cherokees in his name since the Cherokees were not allowed to own their own land. By 1860, a large block of land known as the Qualla Boundary had been purchased. Will Thomas' life was controversial at times. Chief Will Thomas died May 10, 1893 at 88 years old. He left behind the Qualla Boundary and the knowledge that without him, there would have been no Eastern Band of the Cherokee.

By: William Waya Stone

SAUCES AND GRAVIES

BLUE JAY'S VENISON BARBECUE SAUCE
(Phoenix Brand World Champion Barbecue Sauce)

1/4 large onion, minced

4 cloves garlic

3/4 c. molasses

2 c. catsup

1/3 c. vinegar

Sauce

1/3 tsp. Tabasco® Sauce

1/2 tsp. black pepper

1/2 tsp. salt

1/4 c. tomato paste

2-3 Tbs. Liquid Smoke®

1/4 c. Worcestershire®

1/2 c. brown sugar, packed

Cook onions and garlic until transparent. Add rest of ingredients and simmer 20 minutes, stirring constantly. Refrigerate 2-3 days before using. The sauce gets better with age. Marinate cooked venison in sauce. Heat thoroughly.

Mitch Blue Jay and Sarah Autumn Skies Hoffmann

CREAM GRAVY

3 Tbs. drippings

2 1/2 c. milk

3 Tbs. flour

1/2 c. cream

Salt and pepper to taste

Pour all drippings from skillet into a small bowl; measure and return 3 tablespoons to skillet. Stir in flour until well blended. Cook over medium heat 2 to 3 minutes, until bubbly. Gradually add milk and cream. Boil until thick and smooth, stirring constantly. Season with salt and pepper to taste.

HAZEL LODMELL

SUNFLOWER GRAVY

1/4 c. chopped bacon

1 Tbs. cornstarch

3 Tbs. chopped onion

6 Tbs. sunflower meal

2 c. water

Salt

Fry bacon and onion until dark brown. Add sunflower meal, cornstarch, and salt. Cook for a minute, stirring constantly. Slowly add water, while stirring. Lower heat and cook until thick. Add more water if necessary. Use as a sauce for vegetables or mush.

GIBLET GRAVY

Giblets from 1 turkey or chicken
4 Tbs. butter or margarine
2 c. pan drippings or chicken broth
1/2 tsp. salt
2 hard-cooked eggs, chopped

4 c. cold water
4 Tbs. flour
1/2 c. milk of Half-and-Half®
1/2 tsp. pepper

Remove liver from giblets and refrigerate. Place other giblets in saucepan and cover with water. Bring to a boil. Reduce heat and simmer for about 1 hour. Add liver and simmer about 30 minutes. Drain. Cool giblets, chop, and set aside. Melt butter in heavy saucepan and stir in flour. Cook and stir for 3 to 5 minutes or until butter barely turns to a golden brown. Slowly stir in drippings or chicken broth and milk. Continue cooking and stirring until thickened. Season with salt and pepper. Stir in hard-cooked eggs and chopped giblets. Makes 3 cups.

SALSA

11 tomatillos, husked and finely chopped chopped
3/4 c. finely chopped onion chopped
6 jalapeño peppers, seeded, juice

4 large ripe tomatoes, finely

1/2 c. fresh cilantro, finely

1 tsp. freshly squeezed lime deveined, and finely chopped

Toss all ingredients together in a bowl. Allow to marinate 1 hour. Serve cold or at room temperature.

CORNMEAL GRAVY

4 pieces side meat
2 1/2 c. milk

1/2 c. cornmeal

Fry meat. You should have enough grease to cover the cornmeal. Cook until meal becomes a light brown. Add milk slowly. Bring to a boil, stirring constantly. Cook until thickened.

BEAN DIP

8 oz. pinto beans
1 onion, chopped
1 1/2 tsp. cumin
1 c. sour cream

2 cloves garlic, minced
Chopped cilantro, to taste
Dash of cayenne pepper
Olive or canola oil

Soak beans overnight. Rinse beans and cover with water. Bring to a boil and simmer until tender. In a frying pan, add enough oil to cover the bottom of the pan. Sauté onions and garlic. Add beans and spices, mashing as they cook. Remove from heat. Puree in a blender and add sour cream.

GREEN TOMATO SAUCE

Peel and stew green tomatoes until they become a soft, smooth mass. To a gallon of tomatoes, add:

5 c. vinegar
1 c. finely chopped onion
1 Tbs. pepper
1 Tbs. ground mustard

3 c. sugar
1 Tbs. salt
1 Tbs. allspice

Boil all slowly until thoroughly mixed. Can and seal while hot.

Grandmother Dora Lowe

SUN SALSA

2 lbs. fresh tomatoes, chopped
chopped
1/4 c. fresh cilantro, chopped
2 Tbs. olive oil
seasoning
1/4 tsp. pepper
1 c. onion, chopped

1 lb. tomatillos, husked and

1/4 c. fresh basil, chopped
1 - 2 tsp. Goya Adobo®

1/2 tsp. sugar
1 Tbs. red wine vinegar

Mix ingredients together and place in a large jar. Cover the jar with cheesecloth. Place in a sunny spot for 4 hours.

HONEY SAUCE

3/4 c. honey
1/2 tsp. cinnamon
1/4 tsp. salt

2 Tbs. shortening
1 Tbs. butter
1/4 tsp. nutmeg

Combine honey, butter, shortening, and salt with 1 1/2 cups water. Bring to a boil; boil for 5 minutes. Pour over fruit dumplings of your choice. Sprinkle with cinnamon and nutmeg. Bake at 400° F. for 30-35 minutes. Yields 6 servings.

TOMATO GRAVY

6 tomatoes
1 Tbs. Liquid Smoke®
1 Tbs. onion powder
1 Tbs. apple cider vinegar

4 chili peppers
1 tsp. ground mustard
1 large egg, beaten

Boil tomatoes and purée in blender. Mix all ingredients together in large bowl. Serve chilled over meats.
NOTE: Tomatoes can be replaced with 1 20-oz. can tomato purée and 1 tsp. chili powder can be used in place of chili peppers.

CHEROKEE CRANBERRY CATSUP

4 c. cranberries
2 c. water
2 c. apple cider vinegar
1 Tbs. allspice
1 Tbs. celery seed
1 tsp. salt

2 large onions, minced
3 c. sugar
1 Tbs. cinnamon
1/2 tsp. cloves
1 1/2 tsp. pepper
1 1/2 tsp. prepared brown
          or Dijon mustard

Boil cranberries and onion together with water until berries pop. Allow mixture to cool slightly and then transfer to blender. Purée mixture. Return mixture to saucepan and stir in remaining ingredients. Simmer over low heat 30 minutes until thick, stirring occasionally.

SAGE AND MUSHROOM SAUCE FOR PASTA

20 sage leaves, washed and patted dry
sliced
1/4 c. butter
Salt and pepper, to taste
1/2 c. water

1 lb. mushrooms, wiped and

1/4 c. flour
Thin spaghetti

Prepare pasta according to package directions. Drain. Melt 1 tablespoon butter. Add sage leaves and fry until they are crisp. Remove and place on clean paper towels. Melt remaining 3 tablespoons butter. Add sliced mushrooms. Sprinkle with salt and pepper. When mushrooms are slightly toasty, remove and set aside. Mix enough water with flour to form a smooth paste. Set aside. Add about 1/2 cup water to hot pan and use wooden spoon to scrap mushroom bits from bottom of the pan. Heat the water to boiling. Gradually add flour paste and stir until it forms a smooth sauce. Add the mushroom mixture to reheat. Reduce heat and simmer. Spoon mushroom sauce over pasta and garnish by scattering fried sage on top before serving.

MEATS AND MAIN DISHES

BEAR

West Virginia Bear Hunting Season is in the late fall (October-December) when the bear is heavy with fat before hibernation. Most folks who get a bear find that the meat needs to be soaked in marinade to take away some of the "wild" flavor. Traditional marinades include: Indian Vinegar (from maple sap), white vinegar, tomato juice, red wine or strong coffee. In most cases the bear meat is covered with marinade for one to two days and the marinade is then discarded. A few recipes will cook the bear in the marinade. Some folks will parboil the bear meat to take off some of the fat before frying or roasting the meat.

PAN FRIED BEAR STEAKS

Marinate the bear steaks for 2 days then fry on a VERY HOT skillet.

2 lbs. bear steak	1/2 tsp. ground ginger
1 tsp. salt	1/2 tsp. pepper
1 c. flour	1/2 c. shortening

Cut ripened steaks 1 inch thick and pound on both sides with a meat hammer. Mix spices and rub mixture vigorously into both sides of meat. Dredge in flour. Heat shortening in skillet and sear meat on both sides. Lower heat, add 3 tablespoons warm water, and cover skillet. Simmer steaks for 15 minutes, turning once. Test with a fork for tenderness.

BUFFALO BURGERS #1

1 lb. ground buffalo	1/2 can tomato soup
1 tsp. pepper	1 tsp. mustard
1 medium onion	1/4 bottle catsup (small bottle)
1 1/2 c. sugar	1 small can pork and beans

Cut up onions and pepper small and fry along with buffalo meat until done. Mash pork and beans up in a bowl. Mix all of the other ingredients into the mashed pork and beans bowl. Add altogether in a pot and simmer on low for an hour. Skim grease off top and serve on hamburger buns.

Standing Deer (Dalphine Riggs)

BEAR POT ROAST

1 pt. vinegar
3 bay leaves
2 onions, quartered
1/2 tsp. basil
1 c. minced celery
1/2 c. ramps (cut small)
Flour
1 stick butter
1 lg. can sliced mushrooms

2 peppercorns
1 stick cinnamon
1/2 tsp. thyme
1/2 tsp. rosemary
2 lbs. bear meat, cut in cubes
Salt and pepper, to taste
1 pt. water
2 Tbs. Worcestershire® sauce

Combine the vinegar, peppercorns, bay leaves, cinnamon, onions, thyme, basil, rosemary, and celery and pour over the bear meat in a bowl. Marinate in refrigerator for 24 hours. Drain bear meat; strain and reserve the marinade. Cook bear meat in a Dutch oven in small amount of fat until browned. Sprinkle with ramps, salt, pepper, and small amount of flour and add water, reserved marinade, butter, Worcestershire sauce, and mushrooms. Simmer for 2 hours or until the bear meat is tender, adding water as needed. Yield 4 servings.

BEAR STROGANOFF

1 lb. cubed bear meat
1 pkg. brown gravy mix
Rice

1 can cream of mushroom soup
1 pkg. French onion

Cook bear meat until well done; drain excess fat in frying pan. Mix all ingredients with bear meat and bring to a boil, simmer for 30 minutes. Serve over rice or noodles.

BLACK BEAR ROAST

Soak a 5-pound roast in water in refrigerator for a day or two. Place in large slow cooker. Set to "High" temperature. Add water to cover. Salt and pepper to taste. Add a large onion, sliced. Cook until as tender as you like.
NOTE: I cook it for 15 hours. Makes a very moist and tender roast with no gamey taste   Aleta Spring Rain Tenney

BUFFALO BURGERS # 2

1 lb. ground buffalo meat sauce

3 tsp. garlic powder grease

10 shakes of Worcestershire®

2-3 tsp. cooking oil or bacon

Add the Worcestershire sauce and garlic powder to the buffalo burger and mix thoroughly until consistent texture. Let stand 2 hours in the refrigerator (overnight works even better). Prior to cooking, form burgers with pressure—you want them to be as flat as possible to cook through. Preheat skillet with oil or grease hot to sear the burgers. After you have seared both sides, lower the heat and cook at medium heat until the meat is cooked all the way through. If you cook them right, the burgers won't fall apart.   Makes 3-4 burgers

NOTE: Buffalo is naturally low in fat so it does not form burgers well for cooking on a barbecue grill—it tends to crumble and fall apart. This recipe is for cooking in a cast iron skillet and is wonderfully tasty.
Wayne Gray Owl

BUFFALOAF

1 c. fine dry bread crumbs

1/4 tsp. pepper

1/2 tsp. mixed herbs of your choice

1 c. whole milk

1 c. carrots, shredded

1 tsp. salt

1/4 tsp. nutmeg

3 eggs

2 lbs. ground buffalo

Finely chopped celery and onion to taste

1/2 c. hickory-flavored catsup, or may use regular instead

Place crumbs, salt, pepper, nutmeg, herbs in bowl. Add eggs and milk; mix well. Let stand 5 minutes. Slowly blend in chopped buffalo, carrots, celery, and onion. Spread evely in 9x13-inch pan. Spread catsup evenly on top. Bake at 325° for 1 hour or until done. Let stand 5 minutes before cutting.

ROAST POUNDED BUFFALO

5 lbs. buffalo roast

2 lbs. shelled pecan halves

1/2 c. sugar

1 c. warm water

Salt and pepper, to taste

Preheat oven to 350°. Place the roast, lightly seasoned with salt and pepper, in a well-greased roasting pan. Roast for 60 minutes until moderately well done. Remove roast and allow to cool about 30 minutes. Reserve drippings. Lower the oven to 325°. Cut cooked and cooled roast into pieces and pound or run through hand-grinder with coarse blade. Spread coarsely ground or pounded meat into another broad roasting pan. Place the first roasting pan with the drippings back over a low heat and de-glaze the pan juices with 1 cup of warm water, stirring and scraping all meat residue from the pan sides and bottom into the broth. Simmer for about 10 minutes, stirring constantly. Pour broth over the ground meat in the second roasting pan, then sprinkle the meat mixture with the pecan halves. Season overall with sugar, salt, and pepper. Place the meat (second roasting pan) in the 325° oven and roast for 20 to 25 minutes, stirring once to blend completely and serve hot.

BUFFALO MEATLOAF

Line a 9x13-inch pan with foil. Set oven to 350° F. Pour 1 cup tomato juice in pan.

Mix by hand in a large bowl:

2 lbs. ground buffalo

1 egg

1 c. old-fashioned oats

1 large onion, chopped

1 c. tomato juice

2 tsp. salt

1/4 to 1/2 tsp. black pepper

After mixing well, form into 2 loaves and place in pan. Cover meat loaves with tomato sauce or ketchup. Cover with foil and bake for 2 hours.

Aleta Spring Rain Tenney

QUAIL

Dress quail. Put on a stick before the fire, or over hot coals. Roast until very brown. Put browned quail in pot of water and boil until well done. Serve with bread or mush.

STUFFED POSSUM ROAST

1 possum, whole
1/8 c. salt
2 large bay leaves
2 medium onions, sliced
    fine
Pepper to taste

1 qt. cold water
4 or 5 bouillon cubes
3 celery stalks, chopped
1 bag stuffing, any kind is

Soak possum in cold salt water for 12 hours. Rinse meat in cold water; refrigerate about 3 – 4 hours. Preheat oven to 350°. Prepare stuffing according to package directions. Stuff possum cavity with prepared stuffing. Close the possum cavity tightly. Place stuffed possum in roasting pan. Add water, bouillon cubes, bay leaves, celery, onion and pepper. After 2 hours, turn the meat and reduce heat to 300°. Cook for 1 hour or until done.

POSSUM BAKE

1 medium possum

6 medium yams

Season well with salt, black pepper, and cayenne. Add 2 tablespoons vinegar and 1 cup water. Cover and place in refrigerator overnight. Turn 2-3 times. When ready to cook, discard marinade and place possum in pot with 1 quart water. Parboil for about 1-1/2 hours. Remove from pot and place in a shallow baking dish with the legs folded under the possum—Discard broth except for one cup to be used in baking. Slice yams lengthwise. Place yams around possum. Sprinkle 2 tablespoons sugar on yams. Pour 1 cup of liquid from pot over possum. (Remove excess fat first.) Bake in moderate oven (300° F.) until yams are done and 'possum is tender.

RABBIT DELIGHT

1 young rabbit
1 c. broth or water with chicken bouillon cube
1/2 c. mushrooms, chopped
1 Tbs. parsley, chopped
1/2 tsp. salt
2 green peppers, chopped

1 Tbs. fat
1/4 c. lemon juice
3/4 c. orange juice
1 pinch ginger
1/4 tsp. pepper

Cut up the rabbit and brown pieces in fat in a heavy pot. Add broth and other ingredients. Season with salt, pepper, and ginger. Cover and cook slowly until tender.

ROAST RABBIT

1 young rabbit, cleaned weight about 2-1/2 lbs., cut into serving pieces
Salt & black pepper, to taste
2 Tbs. olive oil or corn oil
2 Tbs. butter
1 tsp. ground rosemary
2 Tbs. finely chopped ramps or green onions
1 tsp. minced garlic
1/2 c. fresh or canned chicken broth
1/4 c. finely chopped parsley

Preheat oven to 450° F. Sprinkle rabbit pieces with salt and pepper. Heat the oil and half of the butter in a baking dish. Add the rabbit pieces in one layer. Sprinkle with rosemary. Place the dish in oven and bake 30 minutes. Turn rabbit and continue baking 5 minutes. Sprinkle with onions/ramps and garlic. Bake 5 minutes and add the broth. Bake turning the pieces occasionally about 20 minutes. Stir in the remaining 1 tablespoon butter. Sprinkle with parsley and serve.

PAN FRIED RABBIT

1 stick margarine, divided

2 c. cornmeal or flour

3 c. milk, divided

1 rabbit, cut in small pieces

Melt 1/2 stick of margarine in large fry pan. Dip rabbit pieces in 1 cup milk and then in corn meal or flour.   Place in fry pan. Brown both sides over medium heat (adding remaining margarine as needed for browning). Add remaining 2 cups milk and cover. Simmer for 30 minutes, checking occasionally and adding more milk if needed, until tender. Serve with rice or mashed potatoes and a vegetable.

GROUNDHOG

Clean groundhog and parboil until tender. Remove from pot, sprinkle with salt, red pepper, and black pepper, to taste. Bake before the fire or in oven until brown.

SAUSAGE RAMP CASSEROLE

1 lb. pork sausage

5 c. grated cheese

15-20 ramps

Salt and pepper, to taste

4 eggs

6 c. milk

10-12 potatoes

Crumble sausage and fry. Beat eggs and milk and set aside. In a large baking dish, layer potatoes, sausage, and cut-up ramps. Repeat another layer of potatoes, sausage, and ramps. Pour egg and milk mixture over this. Top with grated cheese. Bake at 350° F. until the potatoes are done. NOTE: You may partially fry the potatoes. This makes the casserole easier to cook. *Phyllis Laughing Raccoon Snead*

NOTE (from another cook): If ramps aren't available, season with garlic and onion powder to suit taste.

SOUTHERN STYLE SQUIRREL

2 squirrels
Flour to roll squirrel in
2 c. water

Salt & pepper, to taste
6 Tbs. vegetable oil

Cut squirrel into frying size pieces, salt and pepper then roll in flour until coated well. Put in skillet of hot oil and fry until golden. Remove squirrel and all of the oil except for 2 tablespoons, then add water and bring to boil. Place squirrel back into the skillet, turn to low heat, cover, and cook for approximately 1 hour.

PUEBLO INDIAN PORK ROAST

1/4 c. vegetable oil
1 1/2 c. chopped onion
3 cloves garlic, minced
4 dried juniper berries, crushed
1/2 tsp. crushed coriander seed
1 bay leaf
4 large ripe tomatoes, seeded and quartered
1 1/4 c. water
2/3 c. cider vinegar
1/2 c. honey
1 Tbs. ground red chile
1 dried medium-hot red chile, crushed
2 tsp. salt
1 oz. square unsweetened chocolate, grated
4 - 5 lbs. pork rib roast

Heat oil in large heavy saucepan and sauté onions over medium heat until soft. Add garlic, juniper berries, coriander seed, and bay leaf. Sauté for 2 to 3 minutes. Add tomatoes, water, vinegar, honey, ground and crushed chile and salt. Simmer, covered, for 30 minutes. Add chocolate and simmer, uncovered for 20 to 30 minutes until thickened. Preheat oven to 350° F. Place roast fat side up in roasting pan and baste generously with the prepared sauce. Roast for 3 hours, basting occasionally with sauce. Serve slices of roast with sauce drizzled over them.

FISH

Fish and other seafood have traditionally been an important part of many Native people's diet. Some tribes netted fish with nets made of natural fibers. Many used spear- and bow-fishing. At night, fish oil lanterns provided light for the fish hunters.

FRIED BASS

2 lbs. bass fillets

1 c. pancake mix

1 c. whole milk

Olive or vegetable oil

Dip bass fillets in milk. Dredge with pancake mix. Fry in hot oil and drain on paper towels.

CATFISH

8 catfish

1 c. flour

Prepared mustard

Bacon fat

Fillet catfish. Wash in cold water and pat dry. Spread mustard on both sides of fillets. Dredge in flour. Fry in hot bacon fat until golden brown.

BLUE CRAB CAKES

6 c. flaked crabmeat

1/2 c. onion, finely chopped

1/4 c. fine yellow cornmeal

1/2 tsp. paprika

1/4 c. dill weed, finely chopped

1/2 c. red sweet pepper, chopped

    roasted and finely chopped

6 eggs, well-beaten

1 c. fine cornmeal

1/2 c. sunflower or peanut oil

1/2 c. parsley, finely chopped

1/4 c. fresh lemon juice

1/4 tsp. white pepper

1 c. celery, finely diced

1/4 c. wild scallions, finely

1/2 c. chicken stock

1 c. corn oil, for frying

Salt, to taste

Heat sunflower or peanut oil in medium-sized cast iron skillet over medium heat. Quickly sauté the onion in the hot oil, stirring often. Add parsley and stir well. Add 1/4 c. yellow cornmeal, stirring continually and cooking for 5 minutes. Remove from heat and cool. In a large bowl, combine the crabmeat, lemon juice, salt, paprika, white pepper, dill weed, celery, pepper, scallions, chicken stock and eggs. Blend thoroughly. Cover and chill for 3 hours. Heat corn oil in a large skillet over medium-high heat until hot. Shape crabmeat mixture into 16 well-proportioned cakes about 3 inches in diameter and about 1 inch thick and dust each side lightly with the remaining 1 cup cornmeal. Ease the cakes, one at a time without crowding, into hot oil. Brown quickly on both sides, cooking for a total of about 15 minutes. Serve hot.

HOT CRABMEAT SPREAD

1 lb. crabmeat, cleaned of shells
1 c. mayonnaise

8 oz. cream cheese
1/2 tsp. Old Bay® seasoning

Mix thoroughly. Spoon into baking dish. Bake at 325° F. until bubbling around edges and heated thoroughly. Serve hot on crackers of choice.

Carla Whitlatch

COLD CRABMEAT SALAD

1 lb. precooked crabmeat or imitation crabmeat
1 Tbs. onion, finely minced
1 stalk celery, finely minced
1/2 c. mayonnaise, or to suit salad consistency preference
Mix ingredients together. Refrigerate. Serve on crackers or make finger sandwiches.

Carla Whitlatch

GRILLED SALMON

6 salmon steaks
Lemon wedges

30 juniper berries
Salt and pepper, to taste

Crush juniper berries and press halfway down in salmon. Grill over coals about 3 minutes each side. Season to taste with salt and pepper. Serve with lemon wedges.

FIRE-BAKED FISH

1 large fish   Salt and pepper, to taste
Butter   Lemon slices

Clean fish. Place lemon in fish and rub all over with butter. Sprinkle with
salt and pepper. Wrap in aluminum foil. Bake on a smooth, flat rock really
close to the fire.
SAFETY NOTE: Long sticks should be used to retrieve packages of fish
from the fire's edge.

TROUT

6 small dressed trout   6 slices bacon
1/2 c. sherry   1/2 c. melted butter
2 Tbs. lemon juice

Salt the inside of the trout. Mix the sherry, melted butter, and lemon
juice. Place trout in pan and cover with marinade. Let stand 1 hour. Wrap
bacon around trout, securing with skewers. Cook over hot fire, basting
frequently, until bacon is crisp.

FIRESIDE TROUT AND LEEKS

4 brook trout   Wild leeks, diced
Potatoes, diced   Salt and pepper, to taste
Butter

Clean fish. Place fish on squares of aluminum foil. Add leeks, potatoes,
salt and pepper. Put a few pats of butter on top. Seal foil. Place at
fireside near hot coals. Cook 1 hour.

NOTE: Coals should not be hot enough to burn fish.

SEAFOOD CORN PUDDING

4 large ears fresh corn
2 Tbs. melted butter
3/4 c. condensed milk
1 1/2 lbs. small shrimp, shelled and de-veined

3 eggs, well beaten
1 tsp. sugar
Salt and pepper, to taste

Preheat oven to 325° F. Grease 1-1/2 quart casserole with butter and sprinkle with cornmeal. Set aside. Grate fresh corn into bowl. In a separate bowl, beat eggs and fold into corn. Add melted butter, sugar, and condensed milk. Blend well. Add shrimp, salt, and pepper. Blend well. Pour into prepared casserole and bake for 1 hour.

CORNBREAD STUFFED TROUT

3 lbs. trout
1 c. cornbread, crumbled
1/2 c. chopped onion
peppers
1/2 tsp. salt
1/4 tsp. pepper
3 1/4 Tbs. melted butter

1 c. soft bread crumbs
1/2 c. chopped celery
2 1/2 Tbs. chopped green

1/4 tsp. fresh sage
1/4 c. cold water

Salt trout and place in well-greased baking pan. Mix bread crumbs, cornbread, onion, celery, green pepper, 1/2 tsp. salt, sage, and pepper. Slowly add water to mixture, tossing to mix. Stuff trout with bread mixture and brush with melted butter. Cover trout with foil. Bake at 350° F. for 1 hour.

POACHED SALMON

6 1-inch cross-cut salmon steaks
and sliced
2 tsp. parsley, minced
1 red pepper, finely diced
Salt and pepper, to taste

6 medium mushrooms, wiped

2 green onions, finely chopped
1 qt. chicken broth
Lemon wedges

Simmer mushrooms, parsley, onions, and red pepper in chicken broth for 10 minutes. Season with salt and pepper to taste. Cool broth. Place salmon steak in large skillet. Cover with broth and simmer for 15-20 minutes. Do not let broth come to a boil. Remove salmon to serving plate. Top with a drizzle of broth and garnish with lemon wedge.

SCRAMBLED EGGS WITH SALMON

6 eggs
1 Tbs. minced chives
1/2 lb. sliced smoked salmon

1/8 tsp. pepper
2 Tbs. butter

Cut salmon in small pieces and set aside. Beat eggs with pepper until foamy. Stir in chives. Melt butter in skillet. Pour eggs into skillet. Add salmon. Cook slowly until the eggs are soft-cooked.

ROAST DUCK

1 1/2 c. blueberries
2 tsp. brown sugar
1 1/4 tsp. pepper
1/4 tsp. nutmeg
4 - 6 wild duck breasts

2 Tbs. white vinegar
1 tsp. salt
1/4 tsp. ground cloves
1 Tbs. vegetable oil

Combine all ingredients except duck in a blender. Purée coarsely. Remove bones from duck breasts, leaving skin intact. Place breasts on a rack in roaster and coat each one with blueberry mixture. Bake at 375° F. for 30 minutes, basting often.

ROAST WILD TURKEY

1 wild turkey, 8 - 10 lbs.
2 small apples, sliced in half
2 ribs celery, sliced
6-8 slices bacon

Salt and pepper, to taste
1 medium onion, cut in half
1 tsp. sage
Melted bacon fat

Preheat oven for 20 minutes at 325° F. Sprinkle turkey inside and out with salt and pepper. Place apple, onion, and celery into the cavity. Sprinkle inside with sage. Pull legs upward and tie them. Turn the wings under the bird and secure with toothpicks. Place turkey, breast up, on a rack in a roasting pan. Cover breast with bacon slices and cheese cloth soaked in bacon fat. Roast 20-25 minutes per pound. Baste often with pan juices.

BLACKFEET VENISON OR ELK SWISS STEAK

3 lbs. meat
Salt & pepper, to taste
3 Tbs. chopped onion
1 c. canned tomatoes

1/4 c. flour
3 Tbs. fat or shortening
1/2 c. chopped celery
1 c. tomato sauce

Cut up the meat for frying and try to get the most tender parts of the animal. Wash it well with salt water and douse it with flour seasoned with salt and pepper. Melt some fat in a skillet and brown both sides of the meat, turning it only once. Add the onions and celery to the skillet and continue to fry. Wait until the last to add the canned tomatoes and sauce. Add a little water whenever necessary.

CANNED VENISON

Requirements: Quart "Mason" jars with lids and rings
                    Pressure cooker or canning kettle

Cut venison into manageable chunks and stuff into the jars leaving about an inch of room at the top. Add 1 Tbs. salt to the top and seal jars. Cook in pressure cooker under 15 pounds pressure for 1-1/2 hours or 3 hours at normal pressure. Let cool and store. This venison is wonderful in stews and chilies.

Tony Simms

GRILLED VENISON BURGERS

1 lb. ground venison
Salt and pepper, to taste
Vegetable or olive oil

3 oz. pork fat back, ground
Seasonings of choice, to taste

Mix the venison, pork fat back, seasonings, salt and pepper. Heat the barbecue grill and rush burgers with vegetable oil or olive oil. Grill about 4 minutes or until meat is done. Add your choice of condiments.

NOTE: Since venison has little fat, you will need to add some extra fat to the meat. Deer fat is not very tasty, so pork fat is recommended.

JERKY

Slice meat very thinly. Do not cut across grain of meat. Hang slices, making sure that there is an air space between each slice on drying racks. Cover at night. When it is dry and hard, it is ready to eat or to be pounded into powder for pemmican. It may also be cooked in water until soft.

PEMMICAN

Pound together dried venison, dried berries, parched corn, and maple sugar. Small cut pieces of fat may be added. This was carried in a gourd or parfleche bag, and was extremely nutritional – small portions sometimes eaten only once a day.

VENISON CASSEROLE

1 lb. ground deer meat
3 or 4 large raw potatoes, peeled and sliced
1 10-oz. can vegetable beef soup
1 8-oz. can cream of mushroom soup
1 small onion, diced
Pepper and garlic salt, to taste

Place sliced potatoes in bottom of casserole dish. Break ground deer meat on potatoes. Add garlic salt, diced onion, pepper and soups. Cover and bake at 325° F. for one hour or until potatoes are done.

MILD VENISON AND BEANS

1 lb. canned venison
1 large can kidney beans
2 cans tomato sauce
2 green peppers
Salt
Pepper

1 large can pork and beans
1 large can yellow butter beans
1 can tomato paste
1 large onion
Garlic powder
1 Tbs. oil

Dice the peppers and onion and sauté them in the oil. When the onions are transparent, add the canned venison and all of the canned beans and tomato products. Simmer for 15 – 30 minutes and spice to taste with garlic, salt, and pepper. This is a mild bean recipe that especially appeals to children.

Wayne Gray Owl

CHIPPEWA PEMMICAN

4 cups dried meat. It can take 1 to 2 pounds per cup depending upon how lean it is. Use only deer or beef. Get it as lean as possible and double-ground from your butcher if you do not have a meat grinder. Spread it out very thinly on cookie sheets and dry at 180° overnight or until crispy. Re-grind or somehow break it into almost a powder.

3 cups dried fruit mixture such as currants, apples, elderberries, blackberries, raisins, or cherries. Grind some and leave some lumpy for texture.

2 cups rendered fat. Use only beef fat. Cut the beef fat into chunks and heat on the stove using medium heat. Tallow is the liquid that can be poured off and strained.

Unsalted nuts and a shot of honey.
Combine all ingredients in a bowl and hand mix. Double bag into 4 portions.
NOTE: The mixture will last a long time without refrigeration.

SPICY VENISON SAUSAGE

3 lbs. deer meat
1 c. minced onion
1 tsp. marjoram
1 tsp. oregano
1 tsp. black pepper
Salt, to taste

1/4 c. bacon drippings
1 c. parsley, chopped
3/4 tsp. coriander
1 tsp. cayenne
1/4 tsp. cumin

Grind venison with coarse blade. Add parsley and onion; mix well. Add remaining ingredients and blend well; regrind mixture. Divide the mixture into twelve parts. Shape each section into 2-1/4-inch by 5-inch sausage patties. Broil or barbecue until brown. Be sure meat is well done. Serve with fry bread.

VENISON PIE

1 1/2 lbs. ground venison
4 Tbs. shortening
1 c. carrots, cooked
3 c. potatoes, mashed
Paprika

1 medium onion, chopped
1 c. beef gravy
1 c. peas
Butter or margarine

Melt shortening in skillet and sauté onions until transparent. Add ground venison and fry until well browned. Drain. Pour venison mixture into a 2-quart casserole dish. Mix in the gravy and add the carrots and peas in alternate layers. Cover mixture with mashed potatoes. Dot with butter and sprinkle with paprika. Bake at 400° F. for 25-30 minutes.

VENISON MEATLOAF

1 lb. ground venison
1 egg
1/2 green pepper, chopped
1 1/2 tsp. salt

1/4 lb. ground beef or pork
1 c. tomato juice
1 small onion, chopped
1/4 tsp. pepper

Combine. Mix well. Place in a meatloaf pan. Bake at 350° F. for 1 hour.

VENISON MEATBALLS

2 lbs. ground venison
2 c. cooked rice
1/2 tsp. pepper
1 oz. soy sauce
1/4 c. water
Prepared spaghetti sauce

2 large eggs, slightly beaten
1 tsp. salt
1/2 tsp. chili pepper
2 Tbs. hickory-flavored
   Barbecue sauce.

Mix all of the ingredients except spaghetti sauce together. Shape into balls. Place balls in roasting pan and cover with spaghetti sauce. Bake at 325° F. until done.

VENISON CHILI

3 lbs. ground venison
6 cloves garlic
5 large green peppers
4 or 5 chili peppers
1 can white beans
2 Tbs. chili powder
1 tsp. cayenne pepper

2 cans tomato sauce
6 large onions
8 red peppers
1 can red kidney beans
1 1/2 tsp. Tabasco® sauce
1 Tbs. cumin
1 tsp. salt

Brown meat, onions, and green peppers in large, heavy skillet. Add remaining ingredients except the beans. Simmer about 1 hour. Add beans with juice and simmer 20 minutes more.

VENISON JERKY

3 pounds venison cut in strips
1/2 c. apple juice
1/2 c. soy sauce
1/2 c. Worcestershire® sauce
2 tsp. Accent®
2 tsp. seasoned salt

2/3 tsp. garlic powder
2 tsp. onion powder
1 tsp. black pepper
1/4 tsp. mustard seeds
1/2 tsp. mustard powder

Place all ingredients in a large glass jar and shake-stir vigorously to mix. Add venison strips and let stand at room temperature for 24 hours. Remove venison. Line oven rack with heavy aluminum foil and crimp foil to catch the juices. Heat oven to 150° F. and bake for 4-6 hours until "crumbly". Wrap strips in paper and store in a cool place.

VENISON STUFFED PEPPERS

2 1/2 c. cooked ground venison
6 mushrooms, sliced
1/4 c. bacon drippings
1/4 tsp. pepper

6 green peppers
2 scallions, sliced
1 tsp. salt

Wash and core peppers. Sauté the rest of the ingredients in bacon drippings. Stuff peppers with mixture and bake 45 minutes at 350° F.

DEER JERKIE

1 1/2 lbs. deer meat
1/3 tsp. pepper
1 tsp. onion powder
1/4 c. soy sauce

1/3 tsp. garlic powder
Dash of red pepper
1/4 c. Worcestershire® sauce

Slice deer meat against the grain. Marinate for 24 hours. Lay out on cookie sheet. Cook 8 to 12 hours with the oven door partly open at the lowest possible heat setting.

Linda Perkins

PEPPERONI

5 lbs. ground beef
2 Tbs. crushed red pepper
1 tsp. fennel seed
1 tsp. Liquid Smoke®
2 tsp. hickory smoke salt

3 heaping Tbs. Morton Tender Quick®
1/4 tsp. garlic salt
1/2 tsp. anise seed
1 tsp. cayenne pepper

1st day -- Mix all ingredients. Cover and refrigerate.
2nd day and 3rd days -- Keep in refrigerator, covered.
4th day -- Roll in long rolls. Place on broiler pan and place on bottom shelf in oven at low warm setting of 150° F. to 200° F. for 8 hours. Turn every hour or so. Will become dry and hard. Slice and eat as desired. May freeze. NOTE: I have used a mixture of ground beef and ground venison.

Russell Lodmell

SEVEN-LAYER CASSEROLE

1 c. uncooked rice
1 small can tomato sauce
1 c. chopped onions and green peppers
1/4 c. water

1 c. whole kernel corn
1/2 c. water
1 lb. hamburger

Brown hamburger in skillet and set aside. In a casserole dish, layer rice and then corn. Pour 1 can of tomato sauce and 1/2 cup water over these layers. Next, layer onions and green peppers followed by browned hamburger. Cover with 1 can of tomato sauce and 1/4 cup water. Bake, covered, at 350° F. for 1 hour, then uncover and bake for 30 minutes.

BREAKFAST CASSEROLE

1-1/2 lbs. frozen hash browns
3 eggs, beaten
2 oz. cheddar cheese, shredded
Salt and pepper, to taste

1 lb. bacon or sausage
2 oz. Velveeta ® cheese
1 can cream of potato soup

Cook the hash browns with the onion until crisp. Fry the bacon or sausage and drain. Mix together in a 13x9-inch baking dish. Add the cheeses, soup, eggs, salt, and pepper. Bake at 350° F. for 30 to 50 minutes.

BACON AND EGG CASSEROLE

1/4 c. margarine, melted
2 c. milk
2 c. unseasoned croutons
6 eggs

2 c. onion/garlic croutons
1 tsp. prepared mustard
2 c. cheddar cheese, grated
10 slices bacon

Cook bacon until crisp. Crumble it. Coat a 9x12x2-inch casserole dish with vegetable spray. Place croutons in casserole and pour margarine over them. Sprinkle grated cheese over all. Mix milk, eggs, and mustard together. Pour over croutons and cheese. Sprinkle bacon over mixture. Bake at 325° F. for 45 minutes. Allow casserole to stand for 15 minutes before serving.

BEAN AND SAUSAGE CASSEROLE

1 10-oz. pkg. frozen lima beans
1 can kidney beans, drained
1 small onion, chopped, drained
1 lb. smoked sausage, cut in 1-inch pieces
2 Tbs. brown sugar, packed
1/2 tsp. dry mustard

1 21-oz. can baked beans
1 15-oz. can great northern beans,

3/4 c. ketchup
1/2 tsp. salt
1/8 tsp. pepper

Heat oven to 400° F. Rinse frozen lima beans with cold water to separate.
Mix lima, baked, kidney, and northern beans, onion and sausage in ungreased
2-1/2 quart casserole. Mix remaining ingredients; stir into bean mixture.
Cover and bake 40-50 minutes or until hot and bubbly.

VENISON ROAST

Slab of venison, about 2-inches thick
1/4 tsp. pepper
1/2 c. flour
1 Tbs. onion, chopped

4 tsp bacon fat
1 Tbs. celery, chopped
1/2 tsp. salt
2 c. water, boiling

Lay venison on board and pound flour into it. Melt fat in a large frying pan
and brown roast in it. Add all the seasonings and 1/2 of the water. Cover
and let simmer for 55 minutes. Pour in remaining water and simmer until
done.

FRY BREAD TACOS

Prepare fry bread from any of the recipes found in the Bread section of this
cookbook. Prepare taco mix by browning ground beef and adding taco spices
to it. Spoon seasoned meat over fry bread. Add grated cheddar cheese,
chopped onion, chopped tomatoes, chopped lettuce, and salsa.

NOTE: Some people prefer to use a venison chili for the seasoned meat
topping.

SURPRISE BREAD-ON-A-STICK

Prepare your favorite fry bread dough. Wrap flattened dough around fully cooked wiener or Lil Smoky® sausage. Fry in hot oil until dough is well cooked.

INDIAN BURGERS

1 lb. ground beef
Water
4 c. self-rising flour
Oil or shortening for frying

1 c. chopped onion
Salt and pepper, to taste
1 – 2 c. flour for kneading

In large skillet, combine beef, onion, and about 1/2 cup water. Cook over medium heat for 10 minutes until beef is no longer pink. Drain off excess liquid and season beef mixture with salt and pepper. Allow mixture to cool while preparing dough.

Place 4 cups flour in large mixing bowl. Make a well in the flour and add 1-1/2 cups water. Gradually mix flour into water to make a soft, sticky dough. Turn out dough onto a floured board. Knead for 3 – 5 minutes. Divide dough into 8 portions. Flatten dough into 5-inch rounds.

Place about 1/3 cup of beef mixture in the middle of the round. Lift edges of dough and pinch to seal overlapping dough to enclose meat filling. Deep fry at 350° F. for 6 – 8 minutes or until golden brown. Drain on paper towels. Serve immediately.

CHICKEN WITH VEGETABLES

4 skinned chicken breast halves
1 Tbs. fresh parsley, chopped
1 tsp crush thyme leaves
1 c. fresh green beans, whole

1 c. chicken broth
1 tsp. dried rosemary
1 large sweet potato, peeled

Cook chicken on top of stove in non-stick skilled until browned. Add the remainder of the ingredients and heat to a boil. Cover and cook on low heat 20 minutes or until tender.

SAUSAGE-STUFFED ZUCCHINI

1 lb. Italian sausage with casing removed
1 stalk celery, chopped
1 egg
1/4 tsp. black pepper
seeded
1 8-oz. can tomato sauce

1 med. onion, chopped
1/3 c. plain dry bread crumbs
1 Tbs. fresh parsley, chopped
4 large zucchini, halved and

Cut zucchini in half lengthwise. Preheat oven to 350° F, In skillet over medium heat, cook sausage until browned and cooked thoroughly. With slotted spoon, remove sausage to a large bowl. Drain off all but 1 Tbs. drippings. Add the onion and celery to skillet and cook 3 minutes. Add cooked onion and celery to sausage. Stir in bread crumbs, egg, parsley, and pepper. Place zucchini on baking sheet and fill evenly with sausage mixture. Spoon tomato sauce over, cover and bake 30 minutes until zucchini is tender and filling is heated through.

WARRIOR'S CASSEROLE

1 lb. ground beef
1 can cream of chicken soup
1 pkg. corn tortillas
Shredded lettuce

10 oz. sharp cheddar cheese
4 tsp. chopped green chilies
1 c. milk
Tomato wedges

Brown meat and drain. Slice 2-inch chunk from cheese; cut into 6 arrows 2-inches X 1/4-inches thick for garnish. Shred remaining cheese. Combine meat, shredded cheese, soup, milk, and chilies. In 2-quart casserole, layer 1 cup meat mixture and 4 tortillas. Repeat layers. Top with remaining meat mixture. Cover and bake at 350° F. for 50 to 55 minutes. Garnish with cheese arrows, shredded lettuce and tomato wedges.

STUFFED BREAD

Fry bread dough
1/4 tsp. marjoram
1/4 tsp. thyme
1 medium green pepper, chopped
Vegetable oil for frying

2 lbs. ground venison
1/4 tsp. rosemary
1 medium onion, chopped
Salt and pepper, to taste

Prepare your favorite fry bread dough. While fry bread is rising, brown meat. Drain. Add pepper, onion, and spices to meat. Sauté for 5 minutes. Flatten
Fry bread into 6-inch circles. Place about 2 tablespoons of meat mixture onto bread. Fold and seal edges. Fry, turning once. Bread should be done and should be light golden brown.

NOTE: Beef, chicken, turkey, or pork can be used. It may be necessary to add a little oil to the skillet because venison is so lean.

MOOSE STEAK

1 lg. moose steak	3 Tbs. bacon drippings
1/2 c. beef stock	1 med. onion, chopped
1/2 tsp. garlic powder	3 Tbs. tomato paste
1/2 c. water	1 c. sliced fresh mushrooms
2 Tbs. all-purpose flour	1/4 c. cream
Dash of paprika	Salt and pepper, to taste

In a small bowl, dilute tomato paste in water. Set aside. In a large skillet, brown steak in drippings on both sides. Add the stock, onion, garlic, and diluted tomato paste. Cover and simmer until meat is tender, about 1 hour. Remove steak from pan. To simmered stock, add mushrooms and cook 1 minute. Thicken mushroom mixture with flour. Slowly, stir in cream. Heat thoroughly. Season with salt and pepper. Pour mushroom gravy over steak and sprinkle with paprika before serving.

ENCHILADAS

12 corn tortillas	1 1/2 c. bean purée
Vegetable oil spray	1 medium onion, chopped
2 cloves garlic, minced thin	1 red pepper, sliced
1 green pepper, sliced thin	1 qt. tomato sauce
1 zucchini or summer squash, diced	2 Tbs. cilantro
1/2 c. shredded cheese	2 Tbs. vegetable oil

Sauté onions, garlic, peppers, and squash in oil until tender and onions are translucent. Add tomato sauce and cilantro. Reduce heat and simmer for 15 minutes. Coat casserole dish with spray and line with 6 tortillas. Spread bean dip over tortillas and top with cheese. Add remaining tortillas. Spoon squash/tomato mixture over tortillas. Cover and bake 1 hour at 350°

DANDELION QUICHE

For crust:
1/3 c. vegetable oil
3/4 c. unbleached flour
1 Tbs. fresh sage
1/4 tsp. pepper

2 Tbs. milk
3/4 c. cornmeal
1/2 tsp. salt

For filling:
1 medium onion, chopped
1 c. grated cheese
dandelion greens
2 eggs
Salt and pepper, to taste

1 tsp. vegetable oil
2 1/2 c. chopped

2 oz. cottage cheese

Preheat oven to 425° F. For crust, mix oil and milk. Add
remaining crust ingredients and stir until a dough forms. Press
dough on bottom and along sides of pie pan or quiche dish. Bake 5
minutes. Remove from oven. While crust is baking, sauté onion in
oil. Place onion in baked shell. Add grated cheese and dandelion
to shell. In blender, purée eggs, cottage cheese, salt, and pepper.
Pour over greens in shell. Reduce heat to 350° F. and bake for 35
minutes until top of quiche is brown.

SWEET CHILI

1 lb. ground buffalo
6 slices bacon
1 clove garlic, crushed
1/4 c. vinegar
1/2 c. Worcestershire® sauce
1 Tbs. Gravy Master®
1/4 c. brown sugar
1 tsp. paprika
1 1/2 Tbs. prepared mustard

1/2 lb. ground pork
1 c. onion, chopped
14 oz. tomato sauce
1/4 c. lemon juice
2 Tbs. steak sauce
2 Tbs. molasses
1 Tbs. chili powder
1 tsp. salt
1/2 tsp. Tabasco® sauce

1 c. pineapple juice

10 drops hot sauce

1 capful Liquid Smoke®, optional

Fry bacon until crisp, reserving drippings. Remove bacon and drain on paper towels. Crumble bacon and set aside. Sauté onion and garlic in reserved bacon drippings until transparent. Remove to a deep pot or dutch oven. Brown meat in drippings. Add meat, bacon, and all other ingredients to pot. Simmer for 2-3 hours, stirring occasionally.

CHIPPEWA BUFFALO AND WILD RICE CASSEROLE

1/2 lb. ground buffalo

1/2 lb. ground pork

1 lb. mushrooms, sliced

1 c. onions, chopped

1/4 c. flour

1/2 c. heavy cream

2 10-oz. cans chicken broth

2 c. wild rice, cooked and

drained

1 pinch dried oregano

1 pinch dried marjoram

1 pinch dried thyme

1 tsp. salt

Black pepper and Tabasco® sauce, to taste

1/2 c. sliver blanched almonds

Preheat oven to 350° F. Sauté buffalo and pork until all the fat coos out into the pan. Remove meat and break it into small pieces. Set aside and keep warm. Sauté mushrooms and onions in the fat and return meat into pan. Put flour and cream into a small bowl and mix until there are no lumps. Stir into meat and vegetables. Add chicken broth and cook until consistency is that of thick soup. Add cooked rice, herbs, and seasonings. Transfer into a 2-quart casserole dish and bake 25-30 minutes. Garnish with almond slivers.

GRILLED CHICKEN

2 sticks margarine

Apple cider vinegar

Black pepper

3 chickens, split into halves

Light grill and allow to heat while preparing grill sauce. To make marinade, place margarine in a small pan. Pour in enough vinegar to cover. Heat over medium heat, just enough to blend margarine and vinegar. Add black pepper and keep adding black pepper until mixture turns black. This requires much black pepper. When the grill is medium hot, place chicken halves over the coals and cook for about 15-20 minutes. Turn chicken over and brush with vinegar mixture. Baste often and generously. Cook until chicken is done.

NOTE: The chicken will get very dark and crispy during the grilling process.

DRIED BEEF

20 lbs. fresh round steak
2 c. salt

1 tsp. saltpeter
1/4 lb. brown sugar

Mix salt, sugar, and saltpeter, mashing out all lumps. Divide this into 3 portions. Cut pieces of meat lengthwise with grain so that slices will be crosswise. These pieces are best if not more than 5 pounds. Rub meat thoroughly with 1 portion of the salt mixture. Place in a large container and cover. On the second and third days, rub meat with a portion of the salt mixture. Turn meat several times a day and let stand for 7 more days. Hang in a warm place to drip. When there is no more dripping, the pieces of meat can be smoked to improve flavor. Wrap in clean muslin bags and hang in a cool place for 6 weeks before it is ready to eat.

VEGETABLES AND SALADS

BAKED FRESH CORN

Cut fresh corn off cob. Place a little pile or layer in center of cornhusk. Fold husk to make a small packet of corn. Bake in a moderate oven until husk is brown.

DRIED CORN

12 ears corn in milky stage

Scrape corn with sharp knife. First, scrape corn to break off kernels. Second, scrape remainder of corn halfway. Third, scrape off rest of kernels. Mash all kernels until milk comes out. Grease loaf pan. Place mashed corn in pan and bake 45 minutes on low heat until all kernels are golden brown. Cool, then cut up and store.

BEAN CAKES

2 or 3 cans assorted beans
3/4 c. milk
2 tsp. salt
Bacon drippings, for frying

1 1/2 c. cornmeal
2 eggs, beaten
3/4 c. thinly sliced green onions

Rinse beans. In a mixing bowl, combine cornmeal, milk, eggs, and salt. Fold in beans and onions. Form mixture into 2-3 inch patties. Fry in large skillet using bacon drippings for 1-2 minutes over medium heat or until golden brown.

BAKED SQUASH

Place squash on hot ashes. Cover with hot coals. Cook 1 1/2 hours. Remove. Cut in half. Remove seeds. Pour syrup over squash.

BATTER-FRIED SQUASH BLOSSOMS

2 - 3 dozen squash blossoms, picked just before they open
1 c. milk
1/2 c. oil
1 Tbs. flour
1/8 tsp. salt
Pepper, to taste

In a shaker jar, combine milk, flour, salt, and pepper. Place squash blossoms in large pan and gently pour the milk-flour mixture over them. Heat the oil in a large, heavy skillet until a drop of water will sizzle. Fry the batter-coated blossoms in the hot oil until golden brown. Drain on paper towels. Serve hot.

BUTTERNUT SQUASH WITH HICKORY NUTS

1 squash - butternut or acorn   1/4 c. maple syrup
1/2 c. chopped nuts   2 Tbs. butter
Salt to taste

Bake whole squash at 350° F. until tender. Cut in half. Remove seeds. Scoop pulp into bowl with salt, half of the butter, and half of the syrup. Mash until smooth. Stir in nuts. Pour in baking dish and top with remaining syrup and butter. Bake at 425° F. for 20 minutes.

ZUCCHINI CASSEROLE

Enough zucchini squash to fill baking dish   2 Tbs. butter or margarine
2 Tbs. flour   2 c. tomatoes, canned or
fresh
1 small onion, diced   1 small green pepper, diced
1 tsp. salt   1 Tbs. brown sugar
Parmesan cheese

Wash but do not peel squash. Place a layer of slices in the bottom of the dish. Melt butter, adding flour. Add tomatoes, onion, and green pepper.

Season with salt and brown sugar. Simmer about 10 minutes. Pour a layer of tomato mixture over squash, then add squash and tomato mixture alternately until dish is full. Top with parmesan cheese and dot with butter. Bake at 350° for 1 hour.

Grandmother Ruth Hicks

CASSEROLE FROM PERU

Boil 8 unpeeled potatoes. Peel, mash, and add 1 Tbs. olive oil and juice from 2 limes. For color, add red pepper. Salt and pepper to taste.

Filling: 1 large can tuna*, drained 2 stalks celery, diced
   1/2 red onion   Mayonnaise or salad dressing

Blend filling ingredients together.

In a flat pan, place half of the cooked potatoes. Add filling. Cover with remaining potatoes and brown in oven. Garnish with fresh parsley, red pepper, or paprika. Serves 6-8.

Note: Avocado, chicken, or salmon may be substituted for tuna.

POTATOES

Potatoes were an important part of the Native American Indian's diet. They were grown throughout most of North and South America. The Inca word for potato is "papa." The Cherokee call it "nunv" and although the translation of the Cherokee words have been questioned, Mary Ulmer Chiltoskey, a scholar of Cherokee culture, writes that one of the seven clans of the Cherokee was the Wild Potato Clan or a-ni-go-da-ge-wi.

CHIPPEWA WILD DRESSING

Parboil 1/2 cup wild rice for 5-7 minutes. Drain, saving liquid. Add rice to ordinary dressing, using rice liquid to moisten.

Dot Vurnovas

CORN AND WALNUTS

2 cans whole kernel corn   1/2 c. or more to taste of walnut pieces
Heat together in a saucepan and serve hot.

Pat Walks Quietly Lowe

DARK RAIN STYLE SHAWNEE HOMINY

2 16-oz. cans hominy, white preferred   1 c. dried currants
Hickory salt or liquid hickory seasoning   1 c. black walnuts
Mix hominy, currants, and walnuts in saucepan. Heavily lace with seasoning.
Heat until the natural hominy liquid is almost gone.

Dark Rain Thom

CREAMED DANDELION LEAVES

1 lb. fresh dandelion leaves   1 qt. water
2 Tbs. butter   1/2 tsp. salt
2 Tbs. flour   1 c. milk
Salt and pepper, to taste

Clean and wash dandelion leaves. Put in a 3-quart saucepan. Add water and
salt. Allow to come to a boil. Lower heat and simmer for 15 minutes.
Remove from heat and drain. Over high heat, melt the butter in a 2-quart
saucepan. Add the flour and work the mixture into a smooth paste. Add
milk to make a smooth, thick cream. Add salt and pepper. Place the
dandelion leaves, well drained, on a cutting board and chop fine. Add the
leaves to the sauce and mix. Reheat if necessary. Serve with meat.

DANDELION SALAD

1/2 c. cream   1/4 c. butter
2 eggs   Paprika
1 Tbs. sugar   Pepper
1 tsp. salt   4 Tbs. vinegar
4 slices bacon   1 c. dandelions

Carefully wash and break up dandelions. Put into salad bowl. Cut up and fry
bacon. Mix with dandelions. Put the butter and cream into saucepan. Melt
over low heat. Beat eggs. Add salt, pepper, sugar, and vinegar. Mix with
warm cream mixture. Cook over low heat, stirring constantly, until dressing
become thick. Pour over dandelions. Mix thoroughly.

FRIED TOMATOES

Sliced tomatoes, green or red
Cornmeal
Bacon grease or oil, for frying

Salt and pepper
1/2 c. diced onion (optional)

Heat grease or oil in skillet until medium hot. Dip slices in cornmeal and fry until golden brown on both sides. Season to taste.

Momma Bishop

HOMINY # 1

1 c. dried hominy
3 c. water
1 c. black walnuts or hickory nuts,   chopped coarsely
1 c. dried currants
Hickory flavoring to taste

Combine water and hominy. Bring to a rapid boil over medium-high heat. Reduce heat to lowest possible setting. Simmer, tightly covered, and let soak at least 45 minutes. Add walnuts and currants. Season to taste. Cook on top of stove or in oven at 300° F. until hominy is tender. It may be necessary to add more water.
Note: I use English walnuts, dried cranberries, or raisins as alternate ingredients.

Maka (Connie Stone)

HOMINY HASH

2 c. strained hominy
Butter

4 eggs, beaten
Salt and pepper, to taste

Melt 1 Tbs. butter in skillet over medium heat. Add hominy and fry until brown. Add eggs and seasonings. Stir until hominy is brown and eggs are done.

IROQUOIS HAZELNUT STUFFED SWEET POTATOES

6 medium sweet potatoes
    chopped
1/3 c. apple juice or cider
1/2 tsp. cinnamon
1/4 c. milk

1 apple, peeled, cored, and

1/4 c. currants
1/4 tsp. nutmeg
6 Tbs. chopped hazelnuts

Preheat oven to 375°. Wash sweet potatoes, wrap in foil, and bake until tender, about 1 hour. Remove from oven and set aside until cool enough to handle. In a medium skillet over medium heat, cook apple in apple juice until softened, about 4 minutes. Stir in currants, cinnamon, and nutmeg. Cover and set aside. Cut a thin slice off the top of each sweet potato and scoop out most of the flesh into a large mixing bowl, leaving about 1/2-inch of the flesh on the insides of the skins. Place potato shells in a baking pan and set aside. Add apple mixture and milk to sweet potatoes and mix well to combine. Fill shells with potato stuffing and sprinkle the top of each sweet potato with a tablespoon of chopped hazelnuts. Bake for 20 minutes or until hot.

SWEET POTATOES WITH CRANBERRY STUFFING

6 medium sweet potatoes
3 Tbs. butter
1 tsp. salt

1 1/2 c. cranberry sauce
1/3 c. brown sugar
1/2 c. chopped nuts

Bake potatoes until tender, about 30 minutes. Peel away skins. Cut potatoes in half lengthwise. Scoop out some of the pulp, saving it. Mix cranberry sauce, sugar, butter, nuts, and salt together. Stuff insides of potatoes with filling. Fasten halves back together with toothpicks. Place potatoes in baking pan. Heap mashed pulp around potatoes and cover with remaining stuffing mix. Bake uncovered at 350° F. for 20 - 25 minutes.

HOMINY # 2

Boil 1 quart wood ashes for 30 minutes. Do not cook in a metal pot. Strain.
Add corn kernels to water. Add more liquid if needed to cover kernels.
Cook until the hulls fall off the corn. Wash until hulls and ash taste are
gone.

INDIAN GREENS

Combine dandelion greens, wild mustard, lamb's quarters, and a piece of
salt pork. Cover with water and boil for about 1 hour. (The greens may be
drained and cooked in grease if you wish).

LEATHER BREECHES (OR BRITCHES)
Leather Breeches were whole green beans. The strings were removed and
the larger beans often snapped into smaller pieces, then strung using a
darning needle and a piece of grocer's twine and hung against the wall behind
the stove to dry. It was common to have 30 or 40 six-foot strands hanging
on the wall at one time. They were later cooked like fresh beans, but you
learned why the odd name.

Bill Talking Leaves Berdine and
Margaret Little Flower Berdine

NOTE: To further preserve our Leather Breeches from hungry insects trying to
survive a cold winter, my grandmother would shake red pepper (cayenne) over
the small snapped dried beans she stored in baskets.   She dried and stored
EVERY bean she could.

Maka (Connie Stone)

LEATHER BRITCHES

Soak dried beans in enough water to cover them for a few hours. Rinse.
Cover with fresh water. Add 1/4 lb. cubed salt meat, pepper and onions.
Bring to boil, then simmer for 3 hours.
Granny Dillon

MAPLE SORGHUM BEANS

6-8 16 oz. cans of assorted beans including navy, kidney, pinto, and black
1 tsp. dried mustard
4-6 strips bacon
1 c. pure maple syrup
1 c. sorghum

Open and drain the cans of beans. May rinse if you desire. Fry bacon until crisp. Crumble and put in baking dish. Add beans, syrup, sorghum, and mustard. Mix well. If more liquid is needed, add additional syrup and sorghum. Cover baking dish. Bake at 300° F. for 2 hours, stirring occasionally. Uncover and bake and additional 30 minutes or until desired thickness is achieved.

IROQUOIS MASHED SWEET POTATOES

3 lbs. sweet potatoes, about 6 medium, peeled and cut in 1-inch chunks
4 Tbs. butter or margarine
2 Tbs. brown sugar
1 tsp. salt
1/4 tsp. coarsely ground black pepper

In a 4-quart saucepan, place potatoes and enough water to cover. Heat to boil over high heat. Reduce heat to low. Cover and simmer 15 minutes or until potatoes are fork tender. Drain. Return potatoes to saucepan. With potato masher, mash potatoes with all other ingredients. Spoon potatoes into a serving bowl.

PUEBLO VEGETABLE DISH

Corn, white kernel preferred   Onions
Squash – summer, crookneck or zucchini   Green Peppers
Cut up onions and pepper. Boil in small amount of water about 15 minutes. Add corn. Heat to boiling. Add slices of squash. Cook until squash is done. Season to taste. Serve hot.

Dot Vurnovas

SUCCOTASH

1 1/2 c. fried corn
1 c. chopped onion
1/2 tsp. chili powder

1/2 c. sunflower seeds
1 1/2 c. cooked lima beans
2 c. chopped tomatoes

Combine ingredients and cook until done, adding water as needed.

CATTAILS ON THE COB

In the spring, green cattails are picked and boiled like corn. Split open the outer shell and eat the seeds off the stalk. The taste is like squash.

CATTAIL POTATOES

A tuber grows at the root of the cattail stalk. These are boiled like potatoes and used in soups and stews.

RELISH

9 green mangoes (peppers)
10 medium sized green tomatoes
3 Tbs. salt
3 c. sugar

9 red mangoes (peppers)
5 medium size onions
4 c. vinegar

Grind vegetables. Add salt. Let mixture set for 1 hour. Then, drain well. Mix vinegar in pan. Heat to boiling. Add vegetables, and let all get hot. Fill jars.

Mary Ann Neal (Windtalker)

WA S DI (RAMPS)

Indians ate ramps long before the white man came to these shores. Some of the Europeans had a similar plant called the ramson and the name carried over in some sections to the sister plant which once grew in our mountains and valleys from southern Ontario to northern Georgia and as far west as Wisconsin.

When you dig ramps, do NOT take all the plants. Dig a few from the patch, move a few feet to one side or the other and dig a few more. Ramps regenerate from the seeds and from the roots. We have been using that method while digging from the same patch for about 30 years now and it is still productive. The old Cherokees dug them by carefully digging around the white stem and cutting it just above the root cluster, leaving the roots in the ground. We don't do it that way. We dig the ramp, cut the root cluster as they did, then replant the clusters. I have tried it both ways and the results are just about the same.

There are several ways to prepare ramps. All methods start with digging the smelly little rascals. Ancient methods included eating them raw with more or less of the soil removed, boiling, steaming, and frying. We have tried them in all those ways, especially fried with either eggs, ham, potatoes, or pepperoni, or a combination of two or more of those additives.

We have two recipes which are a bit unusual. Indians didn't eat them this way because of the time and the availability of at least one of the ingredients.

RECIPE #1 -- Clean ramps thoroughly. Remove fuzzy roots by cutting bulb as close to the roots as possible. Strip any outer layers which form a tough membrane. You should have enough cleaned ramps to fill a 12-inch skillet. Cut one pound of sliced bacon into 1-inch squares. Fry until almost done, then remove pieces from skillet and set aside in a container. You are after the grease at this point. Add ramps to hot grease. Add about 1 cup of cold water. Cover and allow to simmer until ramps begin to turn clear. Remove cover and allow water to evaporate, stirring frequently to prevent scorching. When water in nearly gone, add 1 cup white Vermouth cooking wine and cover until steam from wine permeates ramps. Remove cover. Add back pieces of bacon and continue to fry until ramps begin to turn brown. Serve hot with fried ham, baked potato, and sides.

RECIPE #2 -- FRENCH FRIED RAMPS -- Clean larger bulbs as above. Remove larger leaves so that only an inch or so of leaf remains on bulb. Parboil for about 5 minutes. Drain ramps on paper towels until completely dry. Make a thick batter using complete pancake mix. Dip ramps individually in batter. Drop individual ramps into hot deep fat or oil and fry until golden brown. Do not crowd ramps while frying. Serve hot.

As far as I know, Little Flower originated this recipe. We started taking ramps to Richwood, WV and feeding as many to the old Rampmaster, Jim Comstock, as he could hold. Jim was a ramp-eater from way back and he told us many times (after eating as many as his diet would allow) that he had never tasted ramps as good as the two recipes above.

Little Flower and Talking Leaves

RAMPS CASSEROLE

4 med. potatoes, peeled and thinly sliced
Salt and pepper, to taste
3 c. coarsely chopped ramps, including green tops
1 c. milk
1 (4 oz.) pkg. grated cheddar cheese
1/2 c. fresh bread crumbs
Paprika

Place a layer of sliced potatoes in a greased 1-1/2 quart baking dish. Sprinkle with salt and pepper. Place a layer of ramps on top of potatoes. Continue alternating layers, ending with potatoes on top layer. Pour milk over top. Sprinkle with cheese, bread crumbs and paprika. Bake covered at 425° F. for 20 minutes. Uncover and bake an additional 15 minutes or until potatoes are tender.

WEST VIRGINIA RAMPS

Ramps
Fried bacon
Boiled eggs

Water
Salt and pepper, to taste

Cut cleaned ramps into 1-inch pieces; parboil in plain water. While ramps are boiling, fry bacon in large iron skillet to the point just before they become crisp. Cut bacon in small pieces. Drain parboiled ramps and place in hot bacon fat. Season with salt and pepper to taste and fry until done. Serve garnished with boiled egg slivers. (Ramps are often cooked without boiling. Some cooks break eggs over the ramps during the final seconds of cooking and stir slightly; remove and serve when eggs are done.)

BAKED PIÑON NUTS

Place in a single layer in shallow pan. Bake 3-4 minutes at 350-400 ° F.

Loki Tribbie

RAVEN IN THE SNOW'S INDIAN CORN BAKE

Mix together:
2 eggs, beaten
3/4 stick of butter, melted
1 c. sour cream or French onion dip

Combine:
1 can cream-style corn
1 medium onion (may be omitted if using onion dip)
1 can whole corn
1 medium red or green pepper

Add:
3/4 c. flour
1/4 tsp. garlic salt
1/4 tsp. salt
2 tsp. baking powder
3/4 c. cornmeal
1/4 tsp. chili powder

Mix together, then add:
1 c. grated colby cheese (save a small amount to place on top)

Spoon into a 10" x 13" casserole. Sprinkle cheese on top. Bake at 350° F. for 20 to 25 minutes. Do not over-bake.

Patsy Raven-in-the-Snow Arrington

CHEROKEE CORN PUFFS

20 oz. frozen corn, thawed
1/2 c. flour
1/2 tsp. salt
1/8 tsp. pepper
3 eggs, beaten until light
3 c. oil for frying
1 tsp. baking powder
1/4 tsp. baking soda
1/4 tsp. paprika

Heat oil in kettle slowly. Sift together dry ingredients. Mix in eggs and corn. Drop batter from teaspoon into oil Fry until light and golden on all sides. Drain on paper towels.

WILD GREEN SALAD

Salad:
1 c. wild onions, well chopped
1/4 c. sheep or wood sorrel

4 c. watercress
1 1/2 c. dandelion leaves

Dressing:
1/3 c. sunflower seed oil
3 Tbs. maple syrup
1/4 tsp. black pepper

1/3 c. cider vinegar
3/4 tsp. salt

Toss salad ingredients together. Mix dressing ingredients together and pour over salad. Toss well and serve.

CORN APPETIZER

3 c. shredded sharp cheddar cheese
1/2 c. mayonnaise
1 12-oz. can Green Giant®
   Mexican corn, drained

1/2 c. sour cream
1/4 c. onion
1/2 tsp. salt

Bring cheese to room temperature. Crumble the cheese with a fork or mixer to make small bits. Add all ingredients except corn and blend well. Stir in corn. Chill several hours or overnight.

Wanda Mitchem

DILLY BEANS

2 lbs. trimmed green beans
4 heads dill
1 tsp. cayenne pepper
2 1/2 c. water

1/4 c. salt
4 cloves garlic
2 1/2 c. vinegar

Pack green beans, lengthwise, into hot jars leaving 1/4-inch head space to each pint. Add 1/4 teaspoon of cayenne pepper, 1 clove garlic and 1 head dill. Combine salt, vinegar, and water; bring to boiling. Pour hot vinegar mixture over beans, leaving 1/4-inch head space. Remove air bubbles. Adjust caps, then process pints 10 minutes in boiling water bath.

Carol J. Parker

HARVEST POTATOES

32 oz. hash brown potatoes, frozen
1 can celery soup
1/2 can water
1 c. sour cream
1 stick margarine, melted

2 c. shredded cheddar cheese
1 c. shredded cheddar cheese,
　　for topping
1/2 c. chopped onion

Mix all ingredients, but potatoes and the 1 cup shredded cheese for topping. Add potatoes. Turn into baking dish. Sprinkle with cheese. Bake at 350° F. for 45 minutes to 1 hour.

Cheryl Persinger

CACTUS SALAD

Prickly Pear Cactus
1 turnip, grated
1 c. pecans
1/2 c. vinegar
1 Tbs. basil

1 head lettuce
1 large Bermuda onion
1 c. oil
1 pt. honey
1 Tbs. oregano

Break lettuce up as you would for salads. Grate turnip on lettuce. Cut onion and separate into rings. Add pecans and cactus.
Dressing: Put oil, vinegar, honey, basil, and oregano in container with lid. Shake until mixture is blended. Pour dressing over just before serving, or pour over and let set for a few minutes for a wilted salad.

NOTE: You can get canned cactus at specialty stores that sell Mexican foods or if you have prickly pear cactus plants, you can use it. Drain the canned cactus and run cold water over the cactus to remove some of the liquid. If using fresh plant, first remove the thorns, then place the cactus in boiling water until tender. Cut into strips and place in salad.

June Laughs in the Rain Ford

PRICKLY PEAR CACTUS

Remove thorns from leaves. Slice and boil in water until tender. May be sliced and fried in small amount of fat.

June Laughs in the Rain Ford

BAKED POTATO CASSEROLE

5 large potatoes, cooked and diced crumbled
1 1/2 lb. cheddar cheese, shredded
2 bunches green onion, chopped

6 slices bacon, cooked and

1 pt. sour cream
Salt and pepper, to taste

Sauté onions in bacon grease. Drain. Mix all ingredients together and pour into a casserole dish. Bake 30 minutes at 325° F.

WAYA'S CUCUMBER SALAD

4 - 6 cucumber
separated
1 c. Miracle Whip® salad dressing
Salt and pepper, to taste

1 large onion, sliced and

6-8 packets Equal®
Milk, enough to thin dressing

Peel and slice cucumbers. Add rings of onion. Mix together salad dressing, sweetener, salt, and pepper. Add only enough milk to thin dressing somewhat. Blend into cucumber mixture thoroughly.
NOTE: Add more or less salad dressing and sweetener according to your preferences.

William Waya Stone

MEATLESS BAKED BEANS

1 large onion, chopped
1 Tbs. vegetable oil
1 pkg. vegetarian bacon strips, cut in 1-inch pieces
3 16-oz. cans vegetarian baked beans
1 16-oz. can lima or garbanzo beans, drained
1 16-oz. can kidney beans
1 c. ketchup
2 tsp. Liquid Smoke®
3 Tbs. white or apple cider vinegar
2-4 Tbs. brown sugar
Sauté onion in oil in large skillet. Add bacon and continue to sauté for an additional 3-4 minutes. Set aside to cool. Transfer onion mixture to crock pot. Add beans, ketchup, Liquid Smoke®, vinegar and sugar. Cook on high for 3 hours.
NOTE: The beans may be cooked in a stockpot by simmering for 1-2 hours over low heat.

CORN AND BEANS

Skin flour corn with lye and cook. Cook colored beans. Put the cooked corn and beans together; bring to a boil. Add pumpkin if desired, cooking until the pumpkin is done. Add to this a mixture of cornmeal, beaten walnuts and hickory nuts, and enough molasses to sweeten. Cook this in an iron pot until the meal is done.

SAGE PESTO

1/2 c. olive oil
1 c. fresh sage, firmly packed
1 c. roasted piñon nuts
Juice of 1 lemon

1/4 c. garlic, chopped
1/2 c. fresh parsley
1 tsp. salt
1 Tbs. feta cheese, optional

Place all ingredients in blender and blend until smooth.

RIBBONS OF SQUASH

2 c. mixed unpeeled squash, julienne
1 c. tomatoes
1 Tbs. sage pesto, heaping
Fresh sage leaves

1 c. roasted corn kernels
1 c. mixed beans, cooked
Canola oil

Heat oil in skillet. Add squash, corn, tomatoes, beans, and pesto. Toss quickly. Do not overcook. Place in bowl and garnish with fresh sage leaves. Serve immediately.

HEALTHY NACHOS

24 baked tortilla chips
Chopped green onions
Jalapeño pepper rings
            Low fat sour cream

1/4 c. grated cheddar cheese
Sliced black olives
Bottled salsa

Place chips on a microwavable plate. Sprinkle cheese over chips followed by desired toppings. Microwave 1 minute or until cheese is melted. Serve with salsa, sour cream, and other toppings, as desired.
NOTE: Chips and cheese may be baked in a 350° F. oven for 8 – 10 minutes.

GREENS SALAD

Sweet grass
Ramps
Poke
Bacon grease

Old Field Creases
Angelica
Salt, to taste

Parboil greens. Add salt and grease. Cook until tender. Serve hot.

AUTUMN CASSEROLE

3 c. sliced unpeeled tart apples

1/4 c. brown sugar, packed

1 tsp. cinnamon

1 Tbs. butter or margarine

3 c. sliced carrots, cooked

2 Tbs. flour

1/2 tsp. salt

3/4 c. orange juice

Place half the apples in a greased 2-quart baking dish. Cover with half the carrots. In a bowl, combine brown sugar, flour, cinnamon, and salt. Cut in butter until crumbly. Sprinkle half of mixture over the apples and carrots. Repeat layers. Pour orange juice over all. Bake uncovered at 350° F. for 30 to 35 minutes.

BEAN BALLS

2 c. brown beans

1/2 c. flour

4 c. cornmeal

1 tsp. baking soda

Boil beans in salted water until tender. Put cornmeal, flour and soda in large mixing bow. Mix well. Add boiled beans and some of the bean juice to the cornmeal mixture to form a stiff dough. Roll into balls and drop into a pot of boiling water. Let cook for 30 minutes at a slow boil.

FRESH CORN SALAD

5 c. fresh uncooked corn kernels

1 c. chopped red bell pepper

ginger

  Cooking spray

1 c red wine vinegar

finely

1 Tbs. minced, seeded, jalapeno pepper

1 tsp. salt

1 c. chopped onion

1 Tbs. minced, peeled fresh

2/3 c. chopped fresh cilantro

2 Tbs. green onion, chopped

4 tsp. olive oil

        Black pepper, to taste

Combine corn, onion, red bell pepper, and ginger. Coat a large skillet with cooking spray and warm over medium-high heat. Put corn mixture in skillet and sauté until corn begins to brown. Combine the chopped cilantro and the remaining ingredients in an airtight container and shake well. Combine both mixtures. Cover and chill.

HERB WAX BEANS

1 lb. trimmed wax beans
1 Tbs. fresh lemon juice
1 tsp. salt
1 tsp. dried basil

2 Tbs. slivered almonds
2 Tbs. olive oil
1 tsp. garlic powder
1 tsp. black pepper

Preheat oven to 450° F. Combine all ingredients in a baking pan and mix. Bake for 10 minutes or until beans are browned, stirring occasionally.

GREEN BEAN CASSEROLE

2 9-oz. pkgs. frozen French cut green beans
1/2 c. sliced, canned mushrooms, drained
1 10.5-oz. can cream of mushroom soup
1 tsp. garlic powder
1/2 c. cornflake crumbs

1 1/2 c. chopped onions
1/4 c. water
1 tsp. soy sauce
1/2 c. skimmed milk

Place green beans, onions and water in a microwaveable and oven-safe casserole dish. Cover and microwave on high for 10 minutes, stirring after 5 minutes. Drain when done. In a small bowl, combine milk, soup, soy sauce, and garlic powder. Add the soup mixture to the beans and mix. Top casserole with cornflake crumbs and bake 20-30 minutes at 350° F. until the top is golden brown and beans are tender.

THREE-BEAN SALAD

1/3 c. white vinegar
2 Tbs. white grape juice
1 tsp. celery seed
1 8-oz. can cut waxed beans, drained
drained
1 8 oz. can red kidney beans, drained
1/2 c. green pepper, chopped

2 Tbs. chicken broth
2 Tbs. sugar
1 clove garlic, minced
1 8-oz. can cut green beans,

1/2 c. onion, finely chopped

In a small bowl, combine vinegar, chicken broth, juice, sugar, celery seed, and garlic. In a large bowl, combine beans, onion, and peppers. Add the vinegar mixture and stir. Cover and chill overnight.

POTATO CAKES

1 c. leftover mashed potatoes
1 c. milk
1/2 c. flour
Vegetable oil for frying

2 eggs, beaten
2 tsp. baking powder
1/4 c. minced onion

Add eggs and onions to potatoes and mix thoroughly. Stir in flour and baking powder alternately with milk. Drop from a spoon into hot oil and brown on both sides.

Lissie Lowe

PINTO BEAN CASSEROLE

1 1/2 c. freshly cooked pinto beans, drained
2 green onions, minced
2/3 c. tomatoes, diced
1/2 tsp. dried oregano
2 eggs, beaten
shredded

1/2 c. green pepper, diced
1 tsp. olive oil
1 tsp. chili powder
1/2 tsp. ground coriander
1/4 c. sharp cheddar cheese,

In a large saucepan over medium heat, sauté green pepper and onion in olive oil for 5 minutes or until soft. Stir in the drained beans, tomatoes, chili powder, oregano and coriander. Cook, stirring constantly for 2 minutes. Remove from heat and stir in egg. Coat a 2 cup casserole with vegetable spray. Add the bean mixture and spread evenly. Sprinkle with cheese. Bake at 375° F. for 20 minutes or until filling is set.

CORN KERNELS

3 c. fresh uncooked corn kernels
2 Tbs. white vinegar
1 tsp. salt
1 c. tomatoes, diced and seeded
1 c. green onions, chopped

3 tsp. vegetable oil
1 Tbs. Dijon mustard
1 tsp. pepper
1 c. red bell pepper, chopped

Preheat oven to 425° F. Mix together corn and 1 teaspoon oil in a cake pan coated with cooking spray. Bake for 20 minutes or until browned, stirring occasionally. Mix together 2 teaspoons oil, vinegar, mustard, salt, and pepper in a medium bowl. Add corn mixture, stirring well. Stir in tomato, bell pepper, and onions. Serve warm or at room temperature.

ZUCCHINI SQUASH CASSEROLE

Cooking spray
1 c. grated zucchini
2 Tbs. fresh parsley, chopped
1/8 tsp. salt
2 eggs, beaten
1/4 c. shredded cheddar cheese

1/3 c. chopped onion
1 c. grated yellow squash
1/4 tsp. oregano
1/8 tsp. pepper
1 Tbs. milk

Coat a small skillet or wok with cooking spray. Heat skillet over medium-high heat until hot. Add onion and sauté for 2 minutes. Add zucchini and squash; sauté for 3 minutes. Remove from heat. Stir in half of parsley, oregano, salt, and pepper. Whisk together eggs and milk. Add milk mixture and 3 tablespoons of cheese to squash mixture and stir. Spoon squash mixture into 5x7-inch baking dish which has been coated with cooking spray. Sprinkle with remaining cheese. Bake uncovered at 350° F. for 40 minutes. Garnish with remaining parsley.

GREEN BEANS AND PEPPERS

1 c. chicken broth
1 Tbs. margarine or butter
strips
Salt and pepper, to taste

4 c. fresh whole green beans
1 medium red pepper, cut in

2 Tbs. chopped onion

Wash fresh green beans in cold water and snap off the ends. In a medium saucepan, bring broth to a boil. Add beans and cover. Cook over medium heat 8 – 12 minutes. Melt margarine in a small skillet and add the pepper strips. Sprinkle in the onions. Stir and cook until crisp-tender, about 6 minutes. Drain the green beans. Toss together beans and pepper mixture. Season to taste.

CORN AND TOMATO

1 large green pepper, chopped
1 large carrot, grated coarsely
1 10-oz. can corn
Black pepper, to taste

1 medium fresh tomato, cubed
1 tsp. olive or canola oil
1 Tbs. water

In a saucepan, mix all ingredients and cook for 15 minutes.

BAKED BEAN BARBEQUE

3 c. dried Great Northern beans
1 1/4 c. chopped onion
3/4 c. packed brown sugar
1 Tbs. prepared mustard
1/4 tsp. pepper
strips

8 c. water
1 c. barbeque sauce
1/4 c. molasses
1/2 tsp. salt
4 slices bacon, cut in 1/4-inch

Soak beans overnight. Rinse and drain. Return to Dutch oven. Add water
and onion. Bring to a boil. Cover and reduce heat. Cook 2 hours until beans
are tender. Preheat oven to 350° F. Drain bean mixture and return to pot.
Add remaining ingredients, stirring well. Cover and bake 1 hour.

ROAST CORN

Use dried flour corn. Place about 1-inch of corn kernels in heavy frying pan
(cast iron works best). Heat over medium-low and slowly roast corn, stirring
and turning over to keep it from burning. If the heat is too high, the corn
kernels may explode or blacken. Continue roasting for approximately 30
minutes or until corn is evenly golden brown. Grind roasted corn kernels
using mill or mortar and pestle. A blender can be used, but grinding corn can
soon wear out a blender. A coffee grinder works for small amounts of corn.

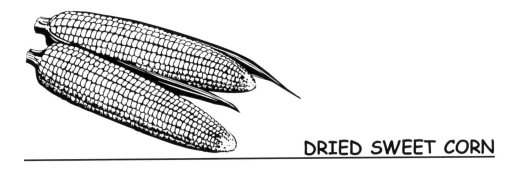

DRIED SWEET CORN

3 qts. fresh corn
1/2 c. sugar
1/4 c. salt

2 Tbs. flour
1/2 c. cream

Cut fresh corn off the cobs. Thoroughly mix together salt, flour, and sugar.
Add dry ingredients to corn and blend. Add cream and mix thoroughly.
Spread corn in thin layers and dry in oven at 250° F, stirring frequently.
When corn is thoroughly dried, store in tight containers.

HULLED CORN FOR HOMINY

1 qt. shelled corn
2 qts. cold water

2 Tbs. baking soda

Wash corn thoroughly. Add soda and water and soak overnight. Bring to a
boil in the same water in which corn soaked. Cook for 3 hours or until hulls
loosen. Add more water as necessary during cooking. Drain off water and
wash corn in clear water, rubbing vigorously until all hulls are removed.
Bring to a boil again in clear water and drain off water. Repeat process
again. Add 1 teaspoon salt to each quart of hominy.
NOTE: Do not use aluminum pot for cooking hominy.

HOMINY CAKES

2 c. cooked hominy
2 eggs
1 c. flour

2 c. milk
3/4 tsp. salt
Vegetable oil for frying.

Cook hominy in salt water until soft. Drain. Add beaten eggs, flour, salt, and
milk. Drop batter from a spoon into hot oil. Fry until brown on both sides.

PEAR AND RASPBERRY SALAD

2 Tbs. raspberry vinegar
1 Tbs. apple juice
Salt and pepper, to taste
1 c. sliced pears
1/4 c. toasted walnuts

2 Tbs. walnut oil
1 Tbs. honey
4 c. mixed baby lettuce
1 c. raspberries

Combine vinegar, walnut oil, apple juice, honey, salt, and pepper in a small bowl and set aside. Place baby lettuce in a large bowl. Toss gently with dressing. Divide lettuce salad onto four salad plates and top with pears, raspberries and walnuts.

Waya (William D. Stone)

CARROT SALSA

1 large carrot, peeled and grated
1/4 c. green chile peppers,
   chopped, roasted, and peeled
1 tsp. lime juice

1/2 red onion, diced
1 clove garlic
2 tomatoes, chopped
1 tsp. salt

Mix all ingredients. Chill before serving.

PIÑON STUFFED MUSHROOMS

3/4 c. white mushrooms
2 Tbs. butter
1 clove garlic, minced
3 Tbs. plain breadcrumbs
1 Tbs. chopped piñon nuts

Fresh lemon juice
3 Tbs. minced onion
1/4 lb. spicy sausage
1 Tbs. minced fresh parsley
Salt and pepper, to taste

Preheat oven to 350° F. Wipe mushrooms clean with a damp cloth. Trim dark ends from mushroom stems. Separate mushroom stems from caps. Chop stems finely and measure out 1/3 cup. Sprinkle caps with lemon juice. Heat butter in medium skillet. Add onion and garlic. Cook, stirring, until onion wilts. Add sausage and cook, stirring until meat is cooked thoroughly. Add chopped stems and cook 3 minutes. Remove skillet from heat. Stir in breadcrumbs, parsley and piñon nuts. Add salt and pepper to taste. Coat a baking sheet with spray. With a teaspoon, fill mushrooms with mixture forming a smooth top. Place on baking sheet and bake for 15 minutes or until golden.

RASPBERRY BEET VINAIGRETTE

8 beets, peeled, cooked and sliced
3 Tbs. raspberry vinegar
1/3 c. olive oil
2 Tbs. chopped chives

2 sweet onion, thinly sliced
2 Tbs. balsamic vinegar
Salt and pepper, to taste

Combine beets and onions in a salad bowl. Mix vinegars in a small bowl. Whisk in oil, pouring it slowly in a steady stream. Add salt and pepper. Toss dressing with beets and onions. Sprinkle with chives.

Waya (William Stone)

FAMOUS MACARONI SALAD

3 or 4 cups cooked macaroni
3 dill pickles, diced
1 small onion, diced
Garlic salt, to taste
Soul seasoning, to taste

6 boiled eggs, diced
1 medium cucumber, diced
1 c. mayonnaise, approximately
Celery salt, to taste

Cook macaroni. Drain and rinse in cool water. Dice eggs, pickles, cucumber, and onion. Stir into macaroni. Add mayonnaise, using enough to give the salad a creamy texture. Add seasonings.

Louise Spirit Dancer Curry

MOM'S SQUASH

2 longneck squash, sliced or sliced

2 large onions, sliced

2 c. cooked corn

12 oz. fresh mushrooms, whole

1/2 c. butter

Sweet potatoes, sliced thin

Melt butter in iron skillet. Brown sweet potatoes. Remove sweet potatoes from skillet and set aside. Put squash in hot butter. Sauté until almost done. Put potatoes back in the skillet. Add other ingredients. Cook until mushrooms are tender. Serve with cornbread.

NOTE: Spirit Dancer and all of her sisters remember this as one of their mother's favorite recipes. In loving memory of Opal Smith.

Louise Spirit Dancer Curry

ZUNI RELISH

2 c. green cabbage, shredded

1/2 c. onions, diced

1 medium onion, diced

1/2 tsp. chili powder

1 Tbs. prepared mustard

1/2 c. carrots, shredded

1/2 c. green pepper, diced

1 Tbs. sugar

1/2 c. apple cider vinegar

1 14-oz. can whole kernel corn

Mix all ingredients well. Refrigerate overnight.

IROQUOIS POTATO SALAD

2 lbs. potatoes

1/2 c. brown sugar

2 Tbs. butter

1 1/2 tsp. salt

1 c. cream

3 large eggs

1/2 c. apple cider vinegar

1 tsp. dry mustard

1/2 tsp. pepper

10 c. water

Wash potatoes, but do not peel them. Put potatoes in water to which 1 teaspoon salt has been added. Bring to boil. Reduce heat and simmer potatoes until done, about 20-25 minutes depending upon size of potatoes. Let potatoes cool and then dice them. Beat eggs with sugar and vinegar. Pour into the top of a double boiler. Add butter, mustard, pepper, and 1/2 teaspoon salt to egg mixture. Cook over slowly boiling water until mixture thickens. Slowly add cream. Pour egg mixture over potatoes and mix well. Refrigerate.

HOPI PEPPER AND ONION RELISH

2 large hot peppers, diced
1 Tbs. salt
14 red apples
1 c. sugar
1 tbs. cinnamon

5 medium onions, finely diced
1 c. boiling water
1 qt. vinegar
1 Tbs. allspice
1 Tbs. cloves

Core apples and dice. Do not peel. Mix diced peppers and onion together. Add salt and boiling water. Let stand 15 minutes. Add apples, vinegar, and sugar. Place spices in a bag made of cheese cloth. Add spice bag to relish mixture and simmer relish for 15 minutes. Discard spice bag. Serve relish hot or cold with meats or cheeses.

BROCCOLI AND WILD RICE

4 c. cooked wild rice
1 onion, chopped finely
Salt and pepper, to taste

2 c. cooked, chopped broccoli
6 oz. cream cheese, softened

Stir together all ingredients in a greased baking dish. Bake at 350° F. for 20-30 minutes.

ZUNI WILTED SPINACH

2 slices bacon
2 green onions, diced
Pepper, to taste
2 cloves garlic, crushed
1/3 c. chili sauce

1/3 c. red wine vinegar
1/2 tsp. oregano
1 tsp. salt
1 Tbs. lemon juice
10 oz. spinach, washed

Cut bacon into small strips. Brown. While bacon browns, place spinach and half of diced green onion in salad bowl. Add vinegar, other half of green onions, oregano, pepper, salt, garlic, lemon juice, and chili sauce in skillet with bacon. Stir rapidly and heat until steaming. Pour over spinach and toss.

GREEN BEANS WITH ONIONS

1 qt. water

8 oz. baby white onions

2 lbs. green beans, cleaned and trimmed

3 Tbs. olive oil

10 cloves garlic, peeled

1/2 tsp. sea salt

2 Tbs. balsamic vinegar

Pepper, to taste

Bring water to boil in saucepan. Drop in onion and let cook 2 – 3 minutes until skins loosen. Strain onions in colander. When cool enough to handle, peel onions with your fingers. Preheat oven to 375° F. In a 9x13-inch baking dish, combine, onions, green beans, and garlic. Sprinkle with salt. Pour olive oil over all and toss to evenly coat vegetables. Bake 20 – 30 minutes, stirring occasionally, until crisp-tender. Remove from oven and drizzle with balsamic vinegar. Season with pepper.

ZUCCHINI CORNSTICKS

1 1/2 c. whole wheat flour cornmeal

1 1/2 c. finely ground

1/2 tsp. sea salt

2 tsp. chili powder

1 tsp. dried dill

2 tsp. baking powder

4 Tbs. canola oil

1 c. milk

1/2 c. apple juice vinegar

1 Tbs. apple cider

1 c. zucchini, shredded minced

1/4 c. green onion,

Preheat oven to 350° F. Sift dry ingredients into a mixing bowl. Add liquid ingredients and stir well with a wooden spoon. Fold zucchini and onion into batter.

Spoon batter into oiled cornstick or muffin pan. Fill 3/4 full. Bake 25 minutes or until tops are light golden brown.

CORN AND SPINACH PUDDING

2 Tbs. butter
1 1/2 c. milk
1 c. cooked, drained spinach
1/2 tsp. nutmeg
1 1/2 tsp. sugar
cheddar cheese
1/2 c. thinly sliced green onions
taste

2 Tbs. flour
2 large eggs, beaten
1 c. corn kernels
1 tsp. salt
3/4 c. grated sharp

Salt and pepper, to

Preheat oven to 375° F. Butter a 1-quart baking dish. In medium saucepan, melt butter and whisk in flour, stirring constantly for 2 minutes. Gradually stir in milk. Simmer until slightly thickened. Remove from heat. Remove about 1/2 cup of milk mixture and stir quickly into beaten eggs. Add egg mixture back into saucepan and blend thoroughly. Stir in spinach, corn, nutmeg, salt, sugar, cheese, onions, salt, and pepper. Pour mixture into baking dish. Bake for 45 minutes or until top is brown and center is firm to the touch. Let cool 10 minutes before serving.

POTATO PANCAKES

3 medium baking potatoes
1 1/2 tsp. salt
finely
1 large egg, beaten
3 Tbs. flour
Vegetable oil

1 c. grated carrot
1 medium onion, minced

1/2 tsp. pepper
1 tsp. baking powder

Peel and grate potatoes and add to grated carrot in a colander. Toss them with salt and let stand over sink for 15 minutes. Squeeze moisture out with your hands. Mix in onion, eggs, pepper, flour, and baking powder until well-combined. Add oil to skillet and place over medium heat. Drop potato batter into the pan by large tablespoons. Flatten with spatula. Brown both sides. Serve immediately.

NOTE: Other vegetables besides carrots can be used. Examples are parsnip, zucchini, winter squash, beets, or turnips.

Althea Simms

Grandmother Moon

Grandmother Moon, send your light
To guide me on the path I have chosen
Send your Power
So that I may conquer my Fears
Send your Strength
So that I may face another dawn
Send your Support
So that I may Stand Alone
Send your Encouragement
So that I may take a step forward
Send me your Heart
So that I may Live again
Sing your lullaby
So that I may Sleep

By Heather Storm Stone

DESSERTS

DRIED APPLES

Dried apples were made by peeling the better apples and cutting them into slices from stem to blossom end. Each apple would make about eight slices, sometimes more. The slices were then strung on grocer's twine using a darning needle as with Leather Breeches and hung behind the stove to dry. We sometimes dried apple wedges in the oven or warming closet. Like the beans, as soon as one batch was dry, another was waiting just off-stage to take its place. The apples were used in pies, fried pies, cakes, and often eaten straight off the string when the chief adult turned her head for a moment.

Little Flower and Talking Leaves

APPLE CRISP #1

Place in greased 9" x 13" cake pan:

6 c. sliced apples

1 tsp. cinnamon

1 c. sugar

1/4 tsp. nutmeg

Mix and pour over apples:

3/4 c. milk

1/2 c. Bisquick®

2 eggs

2 Tbs. vanilla

Mix and crumble over top:

1 c. Bisquick®

1/2 c. chopped nuts

Bake 1 hour at 350° F.

1/2 c. brown sugar

3 Tbs. soft butter

WILD APPLESAUCE

4 lbs. wild crab apples, cored but not peeled, cut in slices

8 oz. maple sugar

4 c. water

Place all ingredients in large saucepan. Bring to boil, and then reduce heat. Simmer 50 minutes, stirring frequently.

OLD-FASHIONED APPLESAUCE CAKE

2 c. sugar
2 1/2 c. flour
1 1/2 c. applesauce
1 c. black walnuts
1/2 tsp. allspice
1/2 tsp. nutmeg (optional)
1/2 tsp. salt

1/2 c. shortening
2 eggs
1 c. raisins
1/2 tsp. cinnamon
1/2 tsp. cloves
2 tsp. baking soda
1/2 c. hot water

Cream shortening. Add sugar gradually. Then add well-beaten eggs. Add applesauce. Sift flour with spices and salt. Mix soda with the hot water. Add the flour mixture alternately with the water. Then, add raisins and nuts, which have been floured. Mix well. Bake in a greased and floured stem cake pan at 350° for 1 hour until a toothpick comes out clean.

Phyllis Laughing Raccoon Snead – "My grandmother was born in 1894 and this was her applesauce cake recipe."

APPLE CRISP # 2

Peel, core, and slice enough apples to fill a 13x9-inch pan. Mix about 1/2 cup flour and enough water to thicken and pour over apples.

Mix: 1 c. white sugar
1 tsp. cinnamon
Pinch of salt
1 c. butter or margarine, softened

1 c. brown sugar
1/2 tsp. nutmeg
1 1/2 c. flour

Mixture will be dry. Spoon over apples. Cover with foil. Bake at 350° F. for 1/2 hour; uncover and bake additional 1/2 hour.

Dianne Rajczak

WILD BERRIES

Pound ripened berries (or fruit) into pulp. Spread on flat surface to dry.
Pulp can be rolled up to store. Add to bread and stews or add to pemmican.
Good to carry on long trips for quick energy.

EASY NO-BAKE COOKIES

4 c. sugar

1 stick butter or margarine

1 c. milk

1/4 c. cocoa

2 c. oats

2 c. coconut

1 c. peanut butter

Mix sugar, butter, milk, and cocoa in heavy skillet or Dutch oven. Bring to
boil. Boil 6 minutes or to soft-ball stage. Take off heat and add remaining
ingredients. Drop onto foil. Let cool.

CREEK BLACKBERRY DUMPLINGS

Part 1 – Combine in pan and let sit.

3 pts. ripe blackberries

1 1/2 Tbs. butter

3/4 c. water

1 c. sugar

Part 2 –

2 c. flour

3 Tbs. sugar

3 1/2 tsp. baking powder

1 tsp. salt

1 egg

Milk

Sift flour, sugar, salt, and baking powder into a bowl. Add egg and mix
well. Add enough milk to make a stiff batter. Place Part 1 on stove and
bring to a boil. Drop dumpling batter a spoonful at a time into boiling
mixture. Cover with lid and cook for about 15 – 20 minutes. Can be served
with cream, ice cream, or whipped cream.

BLACKFEET BERRY UPSIDE DOWN CAKE

4 c. berries
1 c. sugar
1 tsp. vanilla
1 Tbs. baking powder

1/4 c. butter or margarine
2 eggs
1 1/2 c. flour

Mix 3-1/2 cups of the berries with enough sugar to sweeten. Add a couple of tablespoons each of flour and hot water. Pour this mixture into baking pan. Add rest of sugar, flour, eggs, vanilla, and baking powder in bowl and mix well. Pour on top of fruit mixture. Bake at 350° until done. Test with toothpick.

LAKOTA PLUM CAKES

1 c. dark raisins
1 c. boiling water
1 16-oz. can purple plums, drained and pitted
1 c. toasted hazelnuts, chopped fine
1/2 c. melted butter
4 c. sifted all-purpose flour
3 tsp. baking soda
1 1/2 tsp. salt
1 1/2 tsp. allspice
1 tsp. ground cloves
1 c. honey
1/2 c. maple syrup

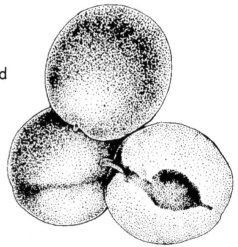

Preheat oven to 350° F. Place raisins in small glass bowl, cover with 1 c. boiling water. Soak 30 minutes until plump. Lightly oil 24 or more muffin cups. Mash plums in a large mixing bowl. Add remaining ingredients to plums and mix well. Add soaked raisins and their liquid. Blend together well. Fill each muffin cup 1/2 full. Bake 30 minutes or until a toothpick inserted in center comes out clean. Cool 10 minutes on wire rack, loosen sides, and turn out of pan. Serve warm with honey or raspberry-plum butter.

MAPLE SUGAR LOLLIPOPS

Simmer maple sugar sap on stove for 3 - 4 hours. Put syrup into a heavy paper cup. Place a stick in the middle and wait until the lollipop hardens. Remove paper from lollipop before serving.

PLAINS CHOKECHERRY CUSTARD

Whole wild chokecherries
Sugar

Water
Cornstarch

Bring chokecherries to a boil, just covering them with water. Mash gently. Strain juice from chokecherries into a pan. Add 1 c. sugar for each pint of juice and 2 Tbs. cornstarch. Heat and stir until thick custard. Serve hot or cold.

NOTE: Plums or other wild fruit may be used to replace chokecherries.

GRANDMA FLORA'S CHEROKEE CORN PUDDIN'

3 cans drained white shoe peg corn
Pinch of cinnamon
1/2 c. sugar
1 can Eagle Brand® Condensed Milk
1 Tbs. vanilla extract

Pinch of nutmeg
Pinch of salt
1/2 pt. heavy cream
4 eggs, beaten
1/4 stick of butter

Try to get all the excess water from the corn. In a saucepan, heat condensed milk , whipping cream and butter . Add in the beaten egg and whip it. Do not boil. Take off the heat and pour the mixture over the corn and add sugar. Beat it a little more. Oven should be preheated to 425° F. Set glass bowl into a baking pan and fill the pan halfway up with water. Sprinkle the nutmeg and cinnamon on the top. Cook for about 45 minutes or until you stick a knife into the center and comes back clean. Should be a light golden brown around the edges. For best taste, do not bake in aluminum pans.

Monica R. Sanowar (Sun Dancer)

POLANTA (CORN MEAL CAKES)

1 lb. cornmeal mush made into 12 rounds.
1/2 stick butter
1/4 lb. dark brown sugar

Melt the butter in a glass dish and put in mush rounds. Turn rounds over to make sure butter is on both sides. Sprinkle brown sugar on rounds then bake in a 250° F. oven for 10 minutes, making sure that not all of the sugar melts off the rounds. Serve warm but not hot.

EagleClaw Parkins

A NI S TA OR KA NA HE NA (CORN MEAL MUSH)

1 c. cold water	1 c. yellow cornmeal

Mix ingredients in bowl.

3 c. boiling water	1 tsp. salt

Choose a large pan in which to boil the mixture. It will expand. Gradually add cold water and meal mixture to boiling water. Watch out for popping so that you don't get burned. Put on lid and simmer for about 45 minutes or until thoroughly cooked. When done, pour into greased loaf pan and chill. Serve with milk and syrup or sugar.

Little Flower and Talking Leaves

FRIED MUSH

Slice cold mush into slabs about 1/2 to 3/4-inch thick. Place in skillet containing enough hot fat or oil so that mush is half-covered. Fry until crisp on one side, turn, and repeat on other side. Serve hot with butter and syrup or with fruit preserves or jelly.

Little Flower and Talking Leaves

PUMPKIN-CORN DESSERT

1 small pumpkin

2 ears corn, cut from cob

1/2 c. whole wheat flour

Sugar or honey

Peel, seed, and slice pumpkin. Cover with water and simmer until tender. While pumpkin is cooking, place corn kernels in pie tin. Bake at 350° F. for 15 minutes. Add corn to pumpkin. Add flour, stirring constantly over low heat until mixture thickens. Add sugar or honey, to taste. Serve hot.

SCRAPPLE

Cornmeal mush

1 full c. shredded cooked pork

Salt and pepper, to taste

Add pork to mixture as soon as mush is cooked. Mix thoroughly. Chill in greased loaf pan. Slice into 1/2-inch slabs and fry as above. Serve with butter and syrup or fruit jam or jelly.

NOTE: You can also add cracklin's to the mixture for a different flavor. Break cracklin's into fine pieces and stir into mixture as with above. Fry and serve hot with butter and syrup.

Little Flower and Talking Leaves

CORNMEAL COOKIES

3/4 c. butter or margarine

3/4 c. sugar

1 egg

1 tsp. vanilla extract

1 1/2 c. flour

1/2 c. cornmeal

1 tsp. baking powder

1/4 tsp. salt

1/2 c. raisins (optional)

Cream together butter and sugar. Add egg and vanilla, mixing until smooth. Add flour, cornmeal, baking powder, and salt. Stir in raisins, if used. Drop dough from tablespoon onto greased cookie sheet. Bake at 350° F. for 15 minutes or until lightly browned. Makes 1 1/2 dozen cookies.

NOTE: Some call these cookies se-lu i-sa u-ga-na-s-da in Cherokee. It is believed the recipe was first found in a book dating back to the 1820's.

POTATO CANDY

1/2 c. mashed potatoes
1 lb. confectioners' sugar
1/2 c. peanut butter

Mix warm mashed potatoes with sifted sugar. Roll out in an oblong shape and spread with peanut butter. Roll up like a jelly roll and cut in slices.

GREEN APPLE PIE

4 c. sliced green apples
1 c. sugar
1/2 tsp. cinnamon
1 two-crust pie shell, unbaked

1/4 tsp. nutmeg
Lemon juice, few drops
Butter or margarine

Place peeled and sliced green apples in unbaked pie shell. Add sugar, nutmeg, lemon juice and a few dabs of butter. Place unbaked top crust on and bake at 350° F.

Robin Night Owl Love

INDIAN PUDDING

6 c. milk
1/2 c. black molasses or sorghum
1/4 tsp. ground ginger
1/4 tsp. ground nutmeg
1/4 tsp. salt, if desired
2 eggs

1 c. yellow cornmeal
1/4 c. sugar
1/4 tsp. ground cinnamon
1/4 c. melted butter
1/4 tsp. baking soda

Preheat oven to 250° F. Bring milk to a simmer and remove it from heat. Combine cornmeal, molasses, sugar, ginger, cinnamon, nutmeg, butter, salt, baking soda, eggs, and half the milk in a mixing bowl. Whisk or blend mixture thoroughly. Stir in the remaining milk and pour the mixture into a well-greased, 2-3 quart baking dish. Bake 5-7 hours, stirring occasionally until firm. Yield 8-12 servings.

PUMPKIN PIE SQUARES

1 c. flour
1/2 c. oatmeal
1/2 c. brown sugar
1/2 c. butter
1 16-oz. can pumpkin
1 can evaporated milk

2 eggs
1/2 tsp. salt
3/4 c. sugar
1 tsp. cinnamon
1/2 tsp. ginger
1/4 tsp. cloves

Combine flour, oatmeal, brown sugar, and butter. Mix until crumbly and press into a 9" x 13" pan. Bake at 350° F. for 15 minutes. Combine pumpkin, milk, egg, salt, sugar, and spices. Beat well. Pour over crust and bake at 350° F. for 40 minutes or until set. Cool and cut into squares. Serve with whipped topping.

SASSAFRAS JELLY

6 roots red sassafras
1 bottle liquid pectin
3 Tbs. sassafras powder

3 c. water
3 c. wild honey

Wash sassafras roots and boil in 3 cups water until water is reduced to 2 cups. Strain liquid into another pot and add pectin. Bring to simmer. Add honey and sassafras powder. Simmer 10 minutes. Pour into hot preserve jars. Cover.

NOTE: Remove bark from sassafras roots and dry, then grate or pound into powder.

RAISIN RICE PUDDING

3 Tbs. uncooked white rice
1 1/2 Tbs. sugar
2 eggs
3/4 tsp. cinnamon

1/2 c. raisins
1 qt. milk
1/2 tsp. salt

Rinse rice well. Add all ingredients except eggs. Separate eggs and beat whites until stiff. Beat egg yolks and fold into rice mixture, then fold in egg whites. Spoon gently into a casserole dish. Bake at 300° F. for approximately 2 hours or until done. Stir frequently during baking. Serve warm.

CHOKECHERRY TREATS

1 lb. dried chokecherries
1 c. sugar

1 c. shortening

Grind chokecherries. Add shortening, and then add sugar. Form into balls about the size of golf balls.

CRANBERRY MUFFINS

1 box yellow cake mix
sauce
1/2 c. pecans, chopped
1/3 c. oil

1 can whole berry cranberry

3 eggs
3/4 c. water

Preheat oven to 350° F. Mix all ingredients. Spoon into muffin cups. Bake about 30 minutes or until toothpick comes out clean.

STRAWBERRIES IN HONEY SYRUP

1 qt. fresh strawberries, washed and stemmed
1/4 c. honey
2 Tbs. Sugar
2/3 c. water

Place honey, sugar, and water in saucepan. Boil rapidly for 5 minutes.
Reduce heat. Carefully drop in whole strawberries. Simmer for 5 minutes.
Turn off heat and let berries cool to room temperature in the syrup. May serve warm or cold, ladling syrup over each portion.

RHUBARB PIE

1 9" double-crust pie shell, unbaked

1 1/2 c. sugar

flour

2 tsp. orange rind, grated finely

1/4 tsp. salt

2 Tbs. butter, cut in small pieces

water

1 Tbs. sugar (optional)

4 c. rhubarb, cut up

3 Tbs. cornstarch, or 1/4 c.

1/2 tsp. nutmeg

3 Tbs. zwieback crumbs

1 egg, beaten with 2 Tbs.

Heat oven to 425° F. In large bowl, mix rhubarb, sugar, cornstarch, rind, nutmeg, and salt. Sprinkle bottom of crust with zwieback crumbs. Add rhubarb mixture. Dot with butter pieces. Moisten rim of pie and weave strips of top crust over each other, attaching firmly at edges. Brush top crust with egg mixture and sprinkle with sugar, if desired. Bake pie 20 minutes. Reduce heat to 350° F. and bake 25 minutes longer or until crust is browned and juices bubble up.

NOTE: I replace 2 cups of rhubarb with 2 cups strawberries.

Waya (Bill Stone)

FEAST DAY COOKIES

2/3 c. plus 1/4 c. sugar

shortening

1 egg

4 1/2 tsp. baking powder

1/2 tsp. anise seed

1/2 c. piñon nuts (pignoli), chopped

2/3 c. lard or vegetable

2 c. unbleached flour, sifted

1/2 tsp. vanilla extract

1/3 c. milk

1 tsp. ground cinnamon

Preheat oven to 350° F. In a mixing bowl, cream 2/3 cup sugar and lard. Add egg and blend thoroughly. Stir in flour, baking powder, vanilla, and anise seed, blending thoroughly. Gradually add milk until a stiff dough is formed. Mix in the piñon nuts. Roll dough out on a lightly floured board to 1/2-inch thickness. Cut into 2-inch cookies with cookie cutter. Sprinkle tops with mixture of the remaining sugar and cinnamon. Bake cookies on a well-greased baking sheet for about 15 minutes, or until golden. Cool on a rack. Makes 2 dozen 2-inch cookies.

NOTE: The cookie recipe is very easy to adapt, and the dough is easy to work with--I roll it out with confectioner's sugar instead of flour.

Delilah Conley

SWEET POTATO COOKIES

1 c. sweet potato, cooked & mashed	3/4 c. brown sugar
1/2 c. sugar	1 egg
3/4 c. margarine	1 1/2 c. flour
1 tsp. baking powder	1/4 tsp. cinnamon
1/2 tsp. nutmeg	3/4 c. quick cooking oatmeal
1 c. pecans or black walnuts	1 c. raisins

Mix butter and sugar together. Add eggs and dry ingredients and then pecans and raisins. Drop by teaspoons. Bake at 350° F. for 10 to 12 minutes

SUNFLOWER CRANBERRY MIX

2 c. raw sunflower seeds	1 c. pine nuts
1 c. raw pumpkin seeds	1 c. raisins
1 c. sweetened, dried cranberries	

Mix all ingredients in bowl and serve.

CHEROKEE YAM CAKES

Stir together:

1 c. cooked, mashed yams	1/2 c. cooking oil
1/2 c. milk	

Sift together:

2 c. flour	2 1/2 tsp. baking powder or
wood ash	
1 1/2 tsp. sugar	1 1/2 tsp. salt

Add flour mixture to yam mixture. Blend lightly with a fork. Turn dough onto a floured board and knead gently about 12 kneading strokes, until smooth. Roll about 1/4-inch thick. Cut into rounds. Place on greased cookie sheet and bake at 425° F. for 10-15 minutes.

CATTAIL POLLEN CAKE

2 c. cattail pollen

4 tsp. baking powder

2 eggs

1 1/2 c. water

2 c. all-purpose flour

1 tsp. salt

1/2 c. evaporated milk

1 Tbs. honey

Combine pollen, flour, baking powder, and salt. Beat eggs lightly. Combine eggs with milk, water, and honey. Beat dry and wet ingredients together very gently. Pour into well-greased pans. Bake at 400° F. for 15 to 20 minutes.

NOTE: Cattail pollen gathers on a long spike that extends from the bulbous brownish fruit. To gather it, bend the stalk over a pan or box and shake the fruit or brush the pollen off the spike.

MA MA'S MOUNTAIN PIE

1 stick butter or margarine

1 c. sugar

1 tsp. vanilla

1 c. self-rising flour

3/4 c. milk

2 c. fresh fruit/berries

Melt butter in bottom of baking dish. Add fruit on top of melted butter. Mix batter and spread evenly over berries. Bake at 350° F. for about 30 minutes or until brown.

Maka

BROWN FOX'S SWEET POTATO PIE

2 c. mashed, cooked sweet potatoes softened

2 eggs

1 Tbs. all-purpose flour

1/2 c. buttermilk

1 tsp. vanilla extract

Hershey's Brand® chocolate chips

2 Tbs. butter or margarine,

1 c. sugar

1/2 tsp. salt

1/4 tsp. baking soda

1 unbaked 9" pie shell

Combine sweet potatoes, butter, and eggs, mixing well. Combine sugar, flour, and salt; stir into potato mixture. Combine buttermilk and soda; add to potato mixture, mixing well. Stir in vanilla. Pour filling into shell. Bake at 350° F. for 1 hour and 10 minutes or until set. While pie cools, melt chocolate and drizzle over the pie, to taste.

Principal Chief Clemenceau Brown Fox Allen

WITCHA HONEY BEE ICING

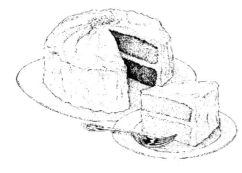

1 c. sugar   1/2 c. honey
3/4 c. marshmallows, chopped   1/3 c. water
1 egg white, stiffly beaten
1/8 tsp. salt
1/2 tsp. vanilla

Combine honey, sugar, water, and salt; place on stove. Boil to 238° F. (soft ball stage) and add marshmallows. Beat and pour into beaten egg white very slowly. Add vanilla and beat until thick and creamy. Good on a variety of cakes.

WILD RASPBERRY CAKE

1 3/4 c. flour   1/2 tsp. salt
1 c. sugar   1 c. raspberries
1 tsp. baking soda   1/2 c. milk
2 eggs, slightly beaten   3/4 c. shortening
1 tsp. cinnamon

Dissolve baking soda in milk. Sift together flour, salt, sugar, and cinnamon. Cut in shortening. Add soda-milk mixture, eggs, and raspberries. Pour into greased pan and bake at 325° F. for 1 hour.

GOOSEBERRY COBBLER

2 c. flour   1/2 c. + 2 Tbs. cornmeal
1/2 tsp. baking powder   1 tsp. salt
3/4 c. butter or margarine   3/4 c. boiling water
2 15-oz. cans sweetened gooseberries   1 tsp. honey
Juice of 1/2 lemon

Sift flour with 1/2 cup cornmeal, baking powder and salt. Cut in butter or margarine. Quickly add the boiling water, mixing well. Divide dough in half and pat half of it in a buttered 8"x8"x2" baking pan. Sprinkle with 1 Tbs. Cornmeal. Mash half gooseberries in their syrup, then stir in remaining gooseberries, honey, and lemon juice. Pour over the dough. Top with remaining dough. Sprinkle with remaining Tbs. Cornmeal. Bake at 425° F. for 30 minutes or until top is lightly browned. Cut into squares and serve.

INDIAN CAKE

4 c. sifted cornmeal
Rounded tsp. lard or butter

3 Tbs. molasses
2 tsp. salt

Mix ingredients and add boiling water until mixture is well moistened. Put into a greased baking pan, smooth surface and bake at 400° F. until well browned.

GRAPE DUMPLINGS

3 c. flour
1 c. sugar
Oil for frying

3 c. grapes
2 Tbs. butter

Mash grapes in a saucepan. Add butter and sugar and bring to a rolling boil. Remove from heat and let cool. Slowly add flour until it turns into a dough. Drop by spoonfuls into hot oil and fry.

MAPLE SUGAR CANDY

1 c, maple sugar
1/4 c. water
Walnut halves

1 c. brown sugar
1/4 tsp. almond extract

Cook sugars and water together to 240° (soft-ball stage). Add almond extract. Cool to lukewarm, then beat vigorously until creamy firm. Knead on cold, smooth surface until smooth. Form into small balls. Press walnut half into each candy.

MAPLE FUDGE

4 c. maple syrup
1/4 c. butter
1 tsp. lemon extract

1 c. whipping cream
1 c. nuts, chopped

Starting cold, cook maple syrup, cream, and butter together at a gentle boil for 9 minutes after boiling point is reached. Remove from heat. Add nuts and lemon extract. Stir vigorously with wood spoon for 5 minutes. Pour into buttered pans. Cut into squares when cool.

UPSIDE-DOWN PUDDING

1 c. maple syrup
1 Tbs. butter or margarine
3 Tbs. brown or maple sugar
1 egg

2 tsp. baking powder
1/4 tsp. salt
1 c. sifted flour
1/2 c. milk

Heat maple syrup to boiling and pour into bottom of buttered baking dish. Cream butter and sugar until fluffy. Sift flour, baking powder, and salt. Add alternately with milk in small amounts, beating well after each addition. Pour batter into hot syrup and bake at 425° F. for 25 minutes. Turn upside-down on serving plate and garnish with chopped nuts and whipped cream.

PUMPKIN ROLL

3 eggs
pumpkin
1 c. sugar
1 tsp. baking soda
3/4 c. flour
2 Tbs. butter or margarine, softened
1/2 tsp. vanilla
dusting

2/3 c. cooked or canned

1 tsp. salt
1/2 tsp. cinnamon
1 8-oz. pkg. cream cheese
1 c. confectioner's sugar
Confectioner's sugar for

Preheat oven to 375° F. Grease a jelly roll pan well and line bottom with waxed paper. Mix eggs, pumpkin, sugar, salt, baking soda, cinnamon, and flour by hand into a batter. Pour batter into prepared pan; spread evenly. Bake 15 minutes. While baking, dust a dish/hand towel with confectioner's sugar. Cool pumpkin cake for 5 minutes; turn into the prepared towel. Remove waxed paper. Roll up pumpkin cake in the towel and tuck in the ends. Refrigerate 1 hour. Prepare filling by mixing cream cheese, butter, 1 cup confectioner's sugar, and vanilla; mix well using mixer. Unroll cake; spread filling over the cake. Separating cake from towel, re-roll and refrigerate.

NOTE: This freezes well.

Donna Martin

OATMEAL COOKIES

1/2 c. margarine
uncooked
3/4 c. brown sugar
2 eggs
1/2 c. flour

2 c. quick-cooking oats,

1/2 tsp. vanilla
1/8 tsp. salt

Heat oven to 400° F. Cream margarine; add sugar. Beat well. Add eggs; beat well. Beat in remaining ingredients. Grease cookie sheet and drop batter by tablespoonful. Bake 8 to 10 minutes.

Heather Storm Stone

HOT MILK CAKE

Cream together:

4 eggs	2 c. sugar

Bring to a boil:

1 stick butter	1 c. milk

Cool slightly.

Blend together:

Egg mixture	Hot milk mixture
2 c. flour	Pinch of salt
1 tsp. baking powder	1 tsp. each lemon, orange, Almond and vanilla extracts.

Bake at 350° F. for 1 hour.

Hazel Lodmell

COOKIES WITH BURNT BUTTER ICING

1/2 c. shortening	1 c. brown sugar
1/2 c. white sugar	2 eggs
1 tsp. vanilla	2-3/4 c. flour
1/2 tsp. baking soda	1 tsp. salt
1 c. chopped nuts	1 c. Carnation® evaporated milk

Mix shortening, sugars, and eggs thoroughly. Stir in milk and vanilla. Mix in salt, flour, and baking soda. Blend in nuts. Chill 1 hour. Bake on greased baking sheet 10 minutes at 375° F.

Burnt Butter Icing –

2 Tbs. Butter	2 c. powdered sugar
1/4 c. Carnation® evaporated milk	

Heat butter in saucepan over medium-high heat until golden brown. Beat until smooth. Add sugar and milk. Spoon over warm cookies.

ZUCCHINI CARROT BARS

1 c. vegetable oil
2 large eggs
1 c. shredded carrots
2 tsp. baking powder
1 tsp. cinnamon
1 c. raisins
1-2 Tbs. frozen orange juice concentrate

1 c. honey
1 c. shredded zucchini
2 c. unbleached flour
1 tsp. nutmeg
1 tsp. ginger
1 c. chopped walnuts

Preheat oven to 350° F. Cream together oil, honey, and eggs until light and fluffy. Add zucchini, carrots, flour, baking powder, spices, raisins, and walnuts, mixing well. Spread into a lightly oiled 13x9-inch baking pan. Bake for 35-40 minutes, until toothpick inserted in center comes out clean. Cool in the pan. Glaze with orange juice concentrate before cutting into bars.

PUMPKIN PIE

Pastry:
1 c. all-purpose flour
4 Tbs. margarine or butter

1/8 tsp. salt
4-5 Tbs. ice water

In a large bowl, combine flour and salt. Using pastry cutter or 2 butter knives, lightly cut the margarine into the flour until the pieces are the size of peas. Add water, a few tablespoons at a time, using fork to mix quickly until pastry forms a ball. Form pastry into a circle about 1-inch thick. Cover with plastic wrap and chill for 1 hour. On a flour board, roll pastry into a circle 2 inches larger than the pie plate. Fold crust in half and lift from board to place in the pie plate. Trim.

Filling:
1/2 c. dark brown sugar, packed
1 tsp. ginger
Pinch of cloves
1 1/4 c. evaporated milk

1 tsp. cinnamon
1/4 tsp. nutmeg
1 16-oz. can pumpkin purée
3 large egg whites

Preheat oven to 450° F. In a large bowl, beat all ingredients until no lumps remain. Pour into prepared pie shell and bake 10 minutes. Reduce heat to 325° F. and bake 50 minutes or until a knife inserted in the center comes out clean.

NOTE: Pumpkin that has been cooked and pureed can be used. To avoid over-browning of pastry, cover edge of pastry with aluminum foil, then remove foil during last 15 minutes of baking.

PUMPKIN AND CRANBERRY CAKE

1/2 c. chopped walnuts
1-1/2 Tbs. toasted wheat germ
1 c. all-purpose flour
1/2 c. toasted wheat germ
1 tsp. pumpkin pie spices
1/4 tsp. baking soda
3/4 c. canned pumpkin
2 Tbs. vegetable oil
1/2 c. sweetened dried cranberries
Cooking spray

3 Tbs. brown sugar
1/4 tsp. pumpkin pie spices
1/2 c. whole wheat flour
2 tsp. baking powder
3/4 tsp. salt
1 c. plain yogurt
1/2 c. packed brown sugar
1 large egg
1 tsp. grated orange rind

Preheat oven to 350° F. Mix walnuts, 3 tablespoons brown sugar, 1-1/2 tablespoons wheat germ, and 1/4 teaspoon spices. Set aside. Combine flours, 1/2 cup wheat germ, baking powder, spices, salt, and baking soda in a deep bowl. Make a well in the center of the flour mixture. Blend yogurt, pumpkin, 1/2 cup brown sugar, oil, and egg, mixing well. Add yogurt mixture to flour, stirring just until moist. Fold in cranberries and orange rind. Spoon batter into a 13x9-inch baking pan that has been coated with cooking spray. Sprinkle walnut mixture over the top. Bake for 25 minutes.

CHERRY JAM
1 qt. cherries, pitted and chopped
1 pkg. powdered pectin
1/4 c. lemon juice
1/4 c. almond liqueur
1/2 tsp. cinnamon
1/2 tsp. cloves
4 1/2 c. sugar

Combine all ingredients except sugar in large saucepot. Bring to a boil, stirring constantly. Add sugar, stirring until dissolved. Return to a rolling boil. Boil 2 minutes, stirring constantly. Remove from heat and skim foam from surface. Ladle hot jam into sterilized jars, leaving 1/4-inch headspace. Secure two-piece caps securely. Process 10 minutes in boiling water bath.

DAMSON PLUM JAM

5 c. damson plum, chopped coarsely   3 c. sugar
3/4 c. water

Combine ingredients in large saucepot. Bring slowly to a boil, stirring until sugar dissolves. Cook rapidly to the gelling point, stirring frequently. Skim foam and ladle into jars. Seal with two-piece caps and process 15 minutes in boiling water bath.

ELDERBERRY JAM

2 qts. elderberries, crushed   6 c. sugar
1/4 c. vinegar

Combine ingredients in large saucepot. Bring slowly to a boil, stirring until sugar
dissolves. Cook rapidly to the gelling point, stirring frequently. Skim foam and ladle into jars. Seal with two-piece caps and process 15 minutes in boiling water bath.

RASPBERRY JAM

2 qts. raspberries   1 pkg. powdered pectin
1/2 c. water   1 Tbs. grated lemon peel
1 Tbs. lemon juice   6 c. sugar

Combine berries, pectin, water, peel, and juice in large saucepan. Bring to a boil over high heat, stirring frequently. Add sugar, stirring until dissolved. Return to a rolling boil. Boil hard for 1 minute, stirring constantly. Remove from heat and skim foam from hot liquid. Ladle hot liquid into sterilized jars and seal with two-piece lid. Process 10 minutes in boiling water bath.

STRAWBERRY JAM

2 qts. strawberries   6 c. sugar

Wash and crush berries. Combine with sugar in large saucepot. Bring slowly to a boil, stirring until sugar dissolves. Cook rapidly until it gels, about 40 minutes. Stir often to prevent sticking. Remove from heat and skim foam from top. Ladle into sterilized, hot jars and seal. Process 15 minutes in boiling water bath.

PUMPKIN CANDY

1 1/2 lb. uncooked pumpkin   2 c. sugar
1 c. fresh lemon juice   Rind of 3 lemons, thinly pared

Cut pumpkin into strips 4x2x1-inch strips. Put strips in bowl and sprinkle with sugar. Add lemon rind strips to the pumpkin and pour lemon juice over. Let the mixture stand 12 hours. Put the mixture in a covered saucepan. Simmer gently until pumpkin becomes translucent, but is still firm, about 1 hour. Remove strips with slotted spoon and drain on paper towels. Let strips dry for 12 hours. Roll them in granulated sugar or eat them plain.

PERSIMMON CHEWS

1 c. dark brown sugar, packed   1 c. uncooked persimmon pulp
1 c. black walnuts, chopped   2 egg yolks
1 Tbs. butter   1/4 c. confectioner's sugar
1/4 c. finely chopped black walnuts

Mix together confectioner's sugar and 1/4 cup finely chopped black walnuts. Set aside. In the top of a double boiler, combine brown sugar, pulp, walnuts, egg yolks and butter. Over boiling water, cook 25 minutes, stirring occasionally. Cool for 1 hour. Form cooled mixture into balls about the size of a walnut. Roll in sugar/walnut mixture. Refrigerate 1 hour before serving.

RICE PUDDING WITH DRIED CHERRIES

1 1/3 c. milk
1 egg
1/2 c. brown sugar
1 Tbs. butter, melted
1/2 c. dried cherries

1 tsp. almond extract
1 egg white
1/8 tsp. salt
1 Tbs. lemon juice
2 c. rice, cooked

Preheat oven to 325° F. Lightly grease a baking dish with lid. Combine milk, almond extract, eggs, sugar, salt, butter, and lemon juice. Beat well. Stir in cherries and rice. Pour mixture into baking dish. Cover and bake 45-50 minutes until set.

NOTE: 1/4 cup honey can be used in place of the brown sugar. Dried cranberries or raisins can be used to replace the cherries.

Melissie Landreth

BAKED APPLES WITH TOPPING

5 Golden Delicious apples
1/4 c. granulated sugar
1/4 c. brown sugar, packed
2 Tbs. plus 2 tsp. extra light olive oil

1 Tbs. granulated sugar
1/4 tsp. nutmeg
1/3 c. all-purpose flour

Prepare apples by peeling, coring, and quartering them. Preheat oven to 350° F. Spray a 13x9-inch baking dish with cooking spray. Toss prepared apples with 1 Tbs. sugar and half of the nutmeg. Layer spiced sweetened apples in baking dish. Combine 1/4 cup sugar, brown sugar, flour and remaining nutmeg in bowl. Drizzle with olive oil and blend with fork, fingers, or pastry blender until crumbly. Sprinkle over apples. Bake about 45 minutes until apples are tender and crumbs are browned.

PUMPKIN BUTTER

3 qts, sugar pumpkin pulp
1 small orange
1 Tbs. ginger
3 Tbs. cinnamon

8 c. sugar
1 Tbs. nutmeg
1 Tbs. cloves

Squeeze juice from orange. Set aside. Grate rind. Set aside. Mix all other ingredients thoroughly in large, heavy saucepot. Cook over medium-low heat until mixture reaches a good spreading consistency. Pour into hot, sterilized jars and seal.

Maka (Connie Stone)

CHEROKEE BREAD PUDDING

2 1/2 c. toasted bread crumbs   2 1/2 c. scalded milk
1 c. butter   1/2 c. sorghum
Pinch of salt   2 eggs, slightly
beaten
1/4 c. currants   1/2 tsp. maple flavoring

Preheat oven to 350° F. Pour milk over bread. Set aside. While bread absorbs milk, heat together sorghum, butter, and salt, mixing to melt butter. Slowly pour sorghum mixture over bread. Cool. Pour bread mixture over eggs. Stir in maple favoring and currants. Pour into a greased casserole dish. Set dish in pan of hot water and bake 50-60 minutes or until firm.

SPIRIT DANCER'S DESSERT

(This is for all of us too-sweet people.)
1 angel food cake
3 pkgs. sugar-free Jello® (orange, cherry, lemon, or lime flavor)
1 12-oz. can lite mixed fruit, drained
1 c. flaked coconut
1 pkg. sugar-free pudding (your choice of flavor)
1 c. chopped nuts, your choice

Crumble cake in bottom of large dish. Prepare first package of Jello® according to directions on package and pour over cake. Refrigerate until firm. Layer mixed fruit over cake layer. Prepare second package of Jello® and pour over fruit. Refrigerate until firm. Sprinkle coconut over fruit layer. Prepare third package of Jello® and pour over coconut layer. Refrigerate until firm. Prepare pudding according to directions and spread over coconut layer. Sprinkle nuts over the pudding and refrigerate until serving.

Louise Spirit Dancer Curry

YAKIMA POACHED BERRIES IN HONEY SYRUP

1 qt. berries

3 Tbs. granulated sugar

1/2 c. honey

2/3 c. water.

Place honey, sugar, and water in small saucepan and boil rapidly for 5 minutes. Reduce heat. Rinse berries. Drop berries in honey mixture and simmer on low heat for 5 minutes. Remove from heat. Allow berries to cool to room temperature in syrup. Serve warm or cold.

YELLOW MAIZE PUDDING

2 1/2 c. cooked corn

1 tsp. vanilla

1 c. evaporated milk

1/2 tsp. nutmeg

Dash of salt

1/2 c. brown sugar

2 eggs

1 tsp. cornstarch

1/2 tsp. cinnamon

3 Tbs. butter

Place corn in saucepan. Grease a 9-inch round baking pan and set aside. Melt butter in small saucepan and set aside. Mix sugar, salt, nutmeg, and cinnamon with corn. Slightly beat eggs and add to corn mixture. Stir well. Put corn mixture over low heat and keep stirring until heated through. Dissolve cornstarch in milk and add to corn mixture. Add vanilla and melted butter. Stir well. Pour into baking pan. Bake at 350° F, for 45 minutes. If knife inserted in middle comes out dry, pudding is done.

CHICKASAW BERRY COBBLER

1 qt. berries

1 c. cornmeal

1 tsp. salt

3 Tbs. butter, melted

1 Tbs. lemon juice

3/4 c. sugar

1 tsp. baking powder

1/2 c. buttermilk

1/4 c. honey

If using large berries such as strawberries, cut them into pieces. Place berries in 2-quart baking dish. Sprinkle with 1/2 cup sugar. Set aside. In small saucepan, place honey, 1 tablespoon butter, and lemon juice. Heat over medium-high heat until butter melts. When melted, pour over berries. Mix thoroughly, yet gently. Mix cornmeal, sugar, baking powder, and salt in bowl. Melt 2 tablespoons butter. Add butter and milk into dry ingredients and stir. Pour cornmeal mixture over berries and bake in 325° F. oven until golden brown.

CHIEF BROWN FOX'S CHOCOLATE SURPRISE

1 can yams   1 6-oz. pkg. chocolate chips

Mash yams and sweeten. Form into balls. Drench is melted chocolate. Refrigerate until firm.

BISCUIT PUDDING

6 biscuits, cold   1 c. hot water
1 1/4 c. sugar   1/4 c. butter or margarine
1 tsp. nutmeg or cinnamon   1/2 c. raisins
2 eggs, slightly beaten   1/2 c. cream or milk

Soak crumbled biscuits in hot water for a few minutes. Add sugar, butter, nutmeg, raising, eggs, and milk, mixing after each addition. Pour into a greased 1-quart baking dish. Bake at 350° F. oven for 30-40 minutes or until browned.

NOTE: Sliced bread can be used in place of biscuits.

Carla Whitlatch

CHEROKEE CORNCOB JELLY

12 ears fresh corn   4 c. water
4 c. sugar   13 fluid oz. package liquid
pectin

Cut corn from cobs and reserve corn for another use. Place cobs in water and bring to a boil. Cover and cook 12-15 minutes. Remove cobs and strain liquid through cheesecloth. In necessary, add water to make 3 cups. Place liquid in saucepan and stir in sugar. Bring to a boil and cook until sugar dissolves. Stir in pectin and cook 1 minute. Remove from heat, skim, and ladle in sterilized jars. Seal with proper lids.

MOM'S NEVER-FAIL FUDGE

4 1/2 c. white granulated sugar
1 stick margarine
chips
1 small jar marshmallow crème
1 tsp. vanilla

1 can condensed milk
12 oz. semisweet chocolate

Nuts, optional

In a large saucepan, combine the stick of margarine, sugar, and milk. Bring to a full rolling boil that cannot be stirred down. Begin to time and allow to full boil (adjust heat down slightly) cook for 9 1/2 minutes exactly. Use a wooden spoon to stir constantly for best results. Stop and remove from heat at the 9 1/2 minute time. Add chocolate chips and marshmallow crème. Whip in air for a couple minutes; then add the vanilla. Stir in nuts and when beginning to thicken, pour into a buttered pan (around a 9x12 depending on the thickness you desire.)

NOTES: Do not use Imperial® margarine because it's too watery. If cooked to the exact time, it turns out every time. Never return to heat once the chips and crème have been added; it will become gritty and bitter if you do.

Sharon Elizabeth Martin shared this
recipe made by her mother, Mary
Evelyn Garrett

BEVERAGES

BLUE CORN BREAKFAST DRINK

1 c. milk
4 tsp. roasted cornmeal
taste

2 tsp. sugar, or to taste
Cinnamon/other spices, to

Add ingredients to milk in saucepan. Stir until combined. Continue stirring over medium heat. Serve steaming hot.

HOMINY CORN DRINK

Corn, field dried or parched
Wood ash lye
Water

Shell the corn (if still on the cob), and soak kernels in wood ash lye until the skin can be slipped off. Remove from the lye and rinse thoroughly with clear water. Drain. Beat the corn in corn beater until it is the size of hominy. Sift the meal from the larger particles. Cook the larger particles in water until they are done. Thicken with a little of the reserved meal. Drink this hot or wait until it sours and drink it cold. It may be kept for quite a while unless the weather is very hot.

HONEY DRINK

1 qt. water   2/3 c. honey

Place water and honey in a large container with tight-fitting lid. Shake well to blend. Chill thoroughly before serving.

SASSAFRAS TEA

Place a quantity of sassafras roots in a large pot. Add 2 quarts water. Bring to a boil. Simmer for 30 minutes. Remove from heat. Let cool, then strain and drink.

NOTE: For those who prefer, it may be sweetened.

JUNIPER TEA

20 tender young sprigs of juniper, washed
2 qts. water

Place sprigs and water in large saucepan. Bring to a boil, then cover and reduce heat. Simmer gently for 15 minutes. Remove from heat and let steep for 10 additional minutes. Strain and serve.

SPICEWOOD TEA

Boil small twigs of spicewood in water and serve hot. Molasses or honey makes the best sweetener.

NOTE: Gather spicewood twigs in the spring when the buds first appear.

SUMAC LEMONADE

Take the red seed clusters of staghorn sumac and boil them in fresh water. Strain through clean cloth and let cool. Try it as is or add sweetener to taste. Maple syrup or maple sugar are suggested.

Phyllis Laughing Raccoon Snead

SUMAC BERRIES

Pick staghorn sumac berries in early September. They can be harvested until a few days after the first frost. Spread berries on a sheet or drying rack in the sun or dry them in an oven on low temperature overnight.   To make tea, do not use leaves and tea should not boil for more than 10 minutes or it will become bitter.   Be certain the berries are harvested from staghorn sumac and not poison sumac. The white fruit of the poison sumac is just exactly as named -- POISON.

WILD MINT TEA

10 large stalks fresh mint, washed
2 qt. water
Place mint and water in large saucepan and bring slowly to a boil. Remove from heat, cover, and let steep for 5 minutes, or until desired strength. Strain and serve.

CRANBERRY JUICE

4 qts. cranberries (either fresh-picked or purchased)
4 qts. water
2-2/3 c. sugar
Cook cranberries in water until skins burst – about 5 minutes. Cook as little as possible because the longer the berries cook the more Vitamin C is destroyed by the heat. Strain through cheesecloth folded or sewn into a jelly bag. Do NOT squeeze the bag or the juice will be cloudy. Let it hang and drip. Add sugar to the juice and heat to 180° F (below boiling.) Place in large, glass jars that have been thoroughly washed and sterilized. Refrigerate.

POSSUM GRAPE DRINK (oo-ni-na-su-ga oo-ga-ma)

Possum grapes, dried   Water
Cornmeal

Shell off grapes from stems. Wash and stew them in water. When they are done, mash them in the cooking water. Let this stand until the seeds settle. Strain. Bring the juice to a boil. Add a little cornmeal to thicken. Continue cooking until the meal is done. Serve hot or cold. Sweeten if desired.
NOTE: Gather possum grapes after the frost has fallen on them. They will be sour. Hang to dry.

UWAGO (oo-wa-ga)

Gather Old Field Apricots. Hull out the seed and pulp, discarding the skins. Put the pulp on to boil. Add a tiny bit of soda to make the seeds separate from the pulp. Mash the pulp and strain it through a cloth. Drink it hot.

NOTE: Old Field Apricots are the fruit of the passion flower.

PINE NEEDLE TEA

Needles, flowers, and candles from yellow pine.

Crush and snip needles, flowers, and pine candles. Bring a pot of water to a boil. Place pine in boiling water, cover, and remove from heat. Let steep for no less than 20 minutes. Tea can be steeped longer, depending upon preference.
NOTE: Yellow pines have 2-5 needles in each cluster. Flower and candles are available only in spring. Tea can be drunk hot or cold. The best tea has a reddish color and a small amount of oil will rise to the top. It can be sweetened with honey if desired. Experiment with proportions to find the tea that meets your flavor preference. Simmering tea rather than steeping it will reduce the vitamin C content.

Around the Lodge

MUD DAUBER TALCUM

Collect mud dauber nests. Break them open and clean out the larvae and other contents. Placed cleaned nests into sack of cotton or other fairly open-weave cloth. Pound with a stone. Pat cloth against baby's bottom for powder. Always remember when making this powder to offer a pinch of the powder to the four winds along with a prayer of thanksgiving for the medicine of the mud dauber.

CABBAGE WORM REMEDY

Punch many holes in bottom of gallon tin can with tight fitting lid. Fill can 3/4 full of slaked lime. Add 2 cups sifted wood ashes and mix thoroughly. Dust cabbages late in the evening or early in the morning when the leaves are damp with dew. Repeat as necessary.

HOMEMADE LAUNDRY SOAP

16 lbs. meat scraps (trimmed fat)   7 1/2 gal. water
3 lbs. caustic soda or lye   2 pints salt

Dissolve caustic soda in water in an iron kettle. Place 1-1/2 gallons of soda solution in a stone jar. Add meat scraps to remaining solution and bring to boiling point. Cook about 2 hours until scraps are dissolved. Add the reserved solution during cooking. Add salt and blend into mixture. Cool mixture. When cold and hard, cut in blocks of desire size and shape.

HOMEMADE LAUNDRY SOAP #2

2 qts. strained grease   1/2 c. ammonia
1 lb. lye   2 Tbs. borax

1 qt water   1/2 c. water

Combine lye and quart of water in stone jar, stirring until lye is dissolved. Set aside to cool. After cool, pour solution over cooled melted grease. Stir until lye and grease are thoroughly combined. Dissolve borax in 1/2 cup water. Add ammonia and borax solution to lye/grease mixture. Stir until quite thick. Pour into an earthenware mold. Let stand several hours, but cut before hard. Put soap in dry place to harden.

RECYCLED SOAP (SORT OF)

When I was a young girl, my mother kept one of those net onion bags hanging in the kitchen near the coal stove and anytime the bar of bath or hand soap was worn down to that thin layer that's nearly impossible to rub across your washcloth to make suds, she'd put the soap in the net bag. Back then, us poor folks didn't use liquid hand soap or scented body wash, so bars of soap were plentiful. On washday, which was usually Friday depending upon the rain, Mother'd use her favorite thin-bladed knife and shave the soap into the steaming tub of water in the old wringer washer. Sometimes, she wouldn't have to add any Tide® until she washed the dirty blue jeans, which was usually the next to last load with the dirty rugs being the last.

Maka (Connie Stone)

STORING RAISINS

Wash raisins in hot water 2 or 3 times. Drain thoroughly, Place a cloth on baking sheet and spread raisins on cloth. Let stand 2 days and then remove the cloth. Bake at 250°F. for 1 hour. Pack in sterilized jars and seal tightly. Raisins prepared in this way will keep for years.

A HELPING HAND

Dry green celery or parsley leaves until crumbly. Store in tightly capped jar to use as seasoning in soups, turkey stuffing, and fillings.

When cookie dough is too soft to handle with ease, place it between sheets of waxed paper that have been floured. Roll atop waxed paper to desired thickness, remove top paper and cut cookies.

Before measuring peanut butter, wipe vegetable oil over inner surface of measuring cup or spoon. Peanut butter will slide out easily.

After cooking and draining rice, place a slice of dry bread on top of rice and cover. Bread will absorb moisture and the rice will be dry and fluffy.

Before discarding empty catsup bottle, pour some vinegar into the bottle and use in making French dressing.

If you don't have buttermilk, add 1 teaspoon vinegar per each 1/2 cup milk.
Lissie Lowe

Before melting chocolate, rub inside of pan it is to be melted in with butter. The chocolate will not stick to the pan.
Pour melted paraffin wax on the cut end of cheese or dried beef to keep it from molding or drying out.

So boiled eggs will peel smoothly, add 1 teaspoon salt to the water as they boil.
Louise Spirit Dancer

To keep muffins from burning around the edges, fill one section of the muffin pan with water instead of batter.

To prevent weeping meringues, beat egg whites immediately before using them. If they are allowed to stand, they "weep" or begin to return to a liquid state.

To prevent onions from burning your eyes when cutting them, first strip back the outer skins, folding them over the root button on the bottom. Holding the onion by the bundle of skin, dice onion by making cross-cuts and slicing. Cut the section immediately above root last.
Chief Virginia Hawk Woman Smith

Wrap whole fish in well-oiled cheesecloth before placing in baking dish. When done, it can be lifted from the dish without falling to pieces. Place on serving platter. Slip spatula beneath fish and slide cloth from beneath.

Stick 2 or 3 pieces of macaroni in the center of the top layer of a double pie crust. The juice will bubble up these "spouts" rather than over the side of the pan.

If a winter storm causes a power outage that lasts longer than a couple of days, use the natural refrigerator outside to keep your frozen foods. If the temperature outside is below freezing or 32° F., take food out of the freezer and place it in coolers outside. Pack snow around the coolers. Watch temperatures closely though. If food thaws, it can spoil quickly.

Wipe clothesline with a cloth soaked in vinegar to prevent wet clothes from sticking to the line on cold days.

Remove chewing gum from chair bottoms, table linens, or your child's hair by massaging the gum with an ice cube. Pick of hard gum in small pieces.

Adding 1 tablespoon of vinegar to the water in which you boil eggs will make peeling them easier.

Grandmother Ruth Hicks

Place a cloth moistened with camphor in the silverware drawer to help prevent tarnishing.

According to my grandmother, after you've thoroughly cleaned your flue, crumple several pieces of waxed paper and burn them. She said the wax would float upward, coating the lower sections of the stovepipe, making it harder for creosote to stick to the slick, waxed surface. Also, she said to periodically burn your potato peelings in a hot fire to reduce creosote accumulation.

Maka (Connie Stone)

Coat the bottom of flowerpots with melted paraffin wax to prevent them from scratching tables or other furniture.

If your basement is dark, paint the bottom step with white paint to prevent accidents.

To remove a spot from the oven caused by spillover from pies or casseroles, let the oven cool, then place a cloth soaked in household ammonia over the spill. Let soak for 2 hours and then rinse.

TO COOK THE BEST-TASTING WILD GAME

Hints to remember:
- Older deer will likely be drier and tougher than younger deer. Vary cooking methods accordingly.
- To make meat tender, cook in some water over very low heat; high heat toughens game and may dry it out.
- Soak meat in salt, vinegar, and water for several hours to remove gamey taste.
- Try various herb blends to season venison. Some that can be combined for a variety of tastes are marjoram, thyme, parsley, or celery flakes. Also try adding onions or garlic.
- Marinades can enhance the flavor of game. Cover the roast or steak in vinegar, wine vinegar, French dressing, Italian dressing, tomato sauce, undiluted tomato soup, tomato juice, pickle juice, orange juice, lemon juice, or grapefruit juice. Be creative!

First Aid in the Spice Rack

Basil -- Insect Bites – crush and apply to bites to pull out poison and relieve pain. Other uses: Place by open window to deter flies. Historical: Basil is a sign of courtship and love in Italy. If a man accepts a sprig of basil from his love, he will adore her forever.

Caraway -- Indigestion – munch on seeds to relieve indigestion. Other uses: greens add licorice flavor to foods

Dill -- Swelling, insomnia in children – Infusion can be used to apply to swellings; water seeds are soaked in can be given to children to sooth into sleep.

Garlic -- High cholesterol; high blood pressure; intestinal parasites; yeast infections – Take in capsules or add raw to foods at the end of the cooking cycle. For animals, add raw garlic or garlic powder to their food to repel fleas and rid them of intestinal parasites. Other uses: mince and soak in water to make a solution to be sprayed on plants to repel Japanese beetles and aphids.

Ginger -- Indigestion, motion sickness – Add ginger to all meat to aid in the digestion. Add to cold water so it doesn't nauseate when drunk on a hot day. Note: Do not use if you have gall bladder disease.

Oregano – Toothache, swellings, headaches – Apply powder to tooth. Infuse for use on swellings.

Parsley -- Edema, arthritis, bad breath -- One of the highest values in vitamin C. Also contains Vitamin A, iron, calcium, thiamin, riboflavin, and niacin.

Peppermint -- Indigestion, muscle spasms, nausea, stuffy noses, headaches
Even peppermint candy will aid.

Rosemary -- Headaches, colic, fever. Other benefits: High in calcium. Other uses: Hair rinse for dark hair.

Sage -- Sore throats, asthma and other bronchial problems, colds. Also used to whiten teeth.

Thyme -- Antiseptic, swellings, bronchial diseases

NOTES ON RESEARCHING YOUR NATIVE AMERICAN ANCESTRY IN WEST VIRGINIA 2014

Wayne Gray Owl.

During a typical week I will get at least a dozen emails and nearly as many phone calls from people who are interested in researching their Native American ancestry. Some are looking to establish their heritage, some are looking for enrollment in a federally-recognized tribe and some are looking to qualify for educational or other benefits. I generally give the same advice:

Start by doing your genealogical tree ignoring for the moment who was Indian, what kind, etc. You may find it difficult to definitely establish tribal linkage using WV records because West Virginia was founded in 1863 as a segregated state and "Indians"- by law did not exist. We were classified as "colored" and it was illegal to register births by Indian tribal identity. In point of fact, it was technically illegal in WV to put American Indian on birth certificates until WV repealed all of the old racial laws in 1965 in response to the 1964 Civil Rights Act. The state Archives in Charleston have the old racial rolls and the US Census data from your Great-grandmother's time may be helpful--The Census data is also available on-line from several sources. Don't be surprised if your relatives are listed as "colored"--also--don't stop if they are on the census rolls as "white"---it was NOT a good thing to be "colored" in WV in those days and there was occasional bribery and fraud to get children listed as white rather than colored. Depending on the county your ancestors lived in, the records at the County Courthouse might be helpful. However, several of the County Courthouses burned in the late 1890s and early 1900s and all of the records for that county were destroyed.

Once you have your genealogy done, you can then begin to identify WHO is Native American and their tribal affiliation. You can THEN determine whether you might qualify for enrollment in a federally recognized tribe or enrollment in AAIWV and whether you qualify for specific benefits. This is where the Tribal Rolls such as the Dawes Rolls, the Baker Rolls, the Old Settlers Rolls come in handy. However, many of the original Tribal Rolls ONLY listed those who were on the Reservation at the time the Rolls were done and may not list people who were not physically on the Rez at that time but who would have qualified for enrollment had they been present. This is where your genealogy comes in—establishing that "granny" was the sister of someone who is on the Rolls may be enough to establish the tribal lineage. You may also find out about your Native American ancestry from other documents,--family bibles, old forms, etc. (I recently had someone send me his father's World War II Draft Card that showed his "Indian" ancestry—but not which tribe).

The information you gather may---or may not--- be sufficient to allow your enrollment in one of the federally recognized tribes or bands. Some folks have definite enrollment requirements that may be hard to meet:

- Some tribes and bands have a specific "blood quantum" requirement—say $1/8^{th}$ or $1/16^{th}$
- Some tribes and bands require that you demonstrate direct descent from someone on the Dawes Rolls (For example, the Cherokee Nation has no blood quantum requirement but does require that you be a direct descendent of someone on the Dawes or Old Settlers Rolls)
- Some tribes and bands are now ONLY enrolling the children of currently enrolled tribal members. For these groups, no documentation is enough to allow your enrollment.

A word of caution, if you are intending to apply for some type of benefits— make sure that you have the appropriate documentation and that you actually qualify for these benefits. Each program is different.

MY FAMILY RECIPES

Made in the USA
Columbia, SC
03 November 2022